ONION GIRL

VIVIENNE MASON

First published by Ultimate World Publishing 2019
Copyright © 2019 Vivienne Mason

ISBN

Paperback - 978-1-925884-83-8
Ebook - 978-1-925884-84-5

Vivienne Mason has asserted her right under the Copyright, Designs and Patents Act 1988 to be identified as the author of this work. The information in this book is based on the author's experiences and opinions. The publisher specifically disclaims responsibility for any adverse consequences, which may result from use of the information contained herein. Permission to use information has been sought by the author. Any breaches will be rectified in further editions of the book.

All rights reserved. No part of this publication may be reproduced, stored in or introduced into a retrieval system, or transmitted in any form, or by any means (electronic, mechanical, photocopying, recording or otherwise) without the prior written permission of the author. Any person who does any unauthorised act in relation to this publication may be liable to criminal prosecution and civil claims for damages. Enquiries should be made through the publisher.

Cover design: Ultimate World Publishing
Layout and typesetting: Ultimate World Publishing
Editor: Hayley Ward
Cover Design: Vivienne Mason

Ultimate World Publishing
Diamond Creek,
Victoria Australia 3089
www.writeabook.com.au

Dedication

To my boys, the lights of my life, if I have done one thing right in this life, it is you. I am proud to be your mother, and you have given me so much joy.

Thanks also to my loving house associate husband for putting up with me, you have been my rock, and I would not be the person I am today, without you.

And finally, in loving memory of Kay, my original soul sister who was at my side throughout our teenage years. I thank you for being my first true friend and am so proud of you for showing me it is okay to break the rules sometimes. Bless you darling, you are a star!

Contents

Dedication iii

Preface vii

Introduction: Do you know your Onions? ix

Chapter 1: Peeling Onions
'Lamia is Awake' 1

Chapter 2: Peeling My Skin
'Onion Girl Speaks' 13

Chapter 3: Peeling Flesh
'Onion Girl breaks free' 19

Chapter 4: Peeling Soul
'Motherhood Calling' 31

Chapter 5: Peeling Responsibility
'Wayward Wife' 41

Chapter 6: Peeling Regret
'Motherhood lost' 59

Chapter 7: Peeling Freedom
'Onion Girl Lets Loose' 73

Chapter 8: Peeling Inner-Self
'Onion Girl's Gypsy Soul' 85

Chapter 9: Peeling Deep Skin
'Inner Child Protection' 105

Chapter 10: Peeling Reality
'Onion Girl Goes Home' 117

Chapter 11: Chopping Onions
'A Celebration' 125

Chapter 12: Onion Girl Sprouts
'New Shoots' 135

Final Words 137

My Menopausal Symptoms 139

Acknowledgements 141

Testimonials 143

About the Author 146

Onion Quotes 148

Onion Tart 150

Preface

Using the metaphor of an Onion, I aim to explore the many layers wrapped around our lives, both consciously and subconsciously.

The time of my life when I hit peri-menopause, when I set off on a journey to Europe, returning to my home in rural England. Leaving my family behind, I ran away from my life in Melbourne, unhappy and feeling overwhelmed. I consistently asked myself four major questions ~ 'What is Home? What is Right Action? What is Love? and Where are all the Wisemen?'

The story is a 'Femoir'. A woman's letter to self about self. An assortment of memories, based on my life and times, but with a smattering of fiction. True events have been chopped like an onion and re-mixed to make a savoury dish.

In my writing style, I have chosen to use letters in respect of my mother who has written to me every week for as long as I can remember. Her wealth of knowledge and wisdom is expressed with love on every page, and I dedicate this format to her and to pay homage to this old-school art.

My friends and family are represented throughout the book, but I have chosen not to identify them but instead have given them new names or nicknames.

ONION GIRL

Nothing I have written is intended to insult or hurt anyone as this story is my own version of events, true or false, and is intended as an expression of myself as Onion Girl.

Happy Reading.

INTRODUCTION

Do you know your Onions?

Peeling each layer, discarding the years of built-up protection and discovering the forgotten version of essential self, stripping back, through stinging tears.
It is time to create.

We live inside our onion, wrapping ourselves up, protecting our inner self with each layer and new life experience. But there comes a time when you need to peel your onion, and for me that was Menopause. This being a part of a woman's life that is unappreciated, unpredictable and misrepresented by many. We are like raw onions with teary reactions, emotional and temperamental, someone to be avoided.

Menopause is like a disease to be treated, and it is a far cry from a celebration of womanhood that it could potentially be. A metamorphosis. Instead, we women stumble blindly into the third age where we are offered hormone HRT patches and quackademic remedies, some of which work wonders for many women every day, and some that don't.

ONION GIRL

People may say *'the change'* makes women crazy, and therefore sympathy and empathy would go a long way in smoothing the rocky road ahead. Indeed, history has seen plenty of women locked away in a Victorian-era institution where they were forgotten by their husbands and mistreated by the staff. How awful it must have been for them.

Writing about my menopause is a little uncomfortable, as it is like my Onion. If I speak of it to the menfolk in my life, I can see they want to back off quickly and return the conversation to familiar subjects like chainsaws and football games. But it is a fact of life and should be embraced as a new beginning. Many women may not even know they are in perimenopause. My own sister had no symptoms whatsoever; she simply stopped having her period. But for me, it was a tumultuous time which led to me peeling my Onion. To get rid of the crusty outer layer of thickened skin that I had grown into and go in search of the person underneath all the layers, the young girl with dreams and aspirations. Instead I was a mother who no longer wanted the responsibilities; if only I could sack myself and break free from all expectations.

With no real experience or role models of women succeeding with their menopause, I struggled with this next stage of a woman's life and shunned the thought of becoming the 'old boiler' stirring the cauldron. Turning 50, I simply was not prepared for the emotional upheaval that was taking place underneath my skin and the many symptoms that created havoc in our daily lives. The hot flushes, itchy skin, bloating, irritability and serious lack of sleep all took their toll on me, until I was raw inside and out.

Cut the onion and you will cry; your eyes will fill with stinging tears as you are left grasping for a tissue. Even the smell of a raw onion can make you recoil, its acrid stench invading the nostrils. But the onion fried will fill the room with tantalising aromas of deliciousness, making a beautiful dish cooked with love, ready to share with your friends and family.

There comes a time when we all have to peel onions.

CHAPTER 1

Peeling Onions

'LAMIA IS AWAKE'

Lamia, you slumbered long and silent beneath my skin, until one moonless night you shifted and uncoiled, body stretching, flexing me awake, I am restless.

Unable to return to my sweet dreams and feeling frustrated, I stretch my aching legs and stumble to the kitchen. The house silent, apart from the fridge humming loudly. Funny how I never noticed this annoying noise before. It is dark. I creep to the sofa and make myself comfortable. It is going to be another long night, and I want to cry. Why can't I stay asleep and be snuggled in my bed like most people? Why do my legs itch and spasm uncontrollably? And why is there is a swarm of bees buzzing in my belly?

My head is full of uncontrollable thoughts, like wild horses, charging around the paddocks. I am hot like a volcano, yet cold to touch. This is the start of my menopause, and for a lot of women the restlessness leaves us irritable and sleep-deprived. Each night it feels like an eternal doom.

ONION GIRL

I wrote a poem for Lamia, who I named my menopause after, in honour of this ancient being. A mythical creature, half woman, half snake who has been known to seek revenge and kill small children in their sleep. She is a beguiling seductress who lures unsuspecting men with her silky sweetness for She is a beautiful demon.

During the months to come, Lamia wrought havoc on my mind, body and soul, upturning tables, and kicking down doors. Screeching obscenities at the traffic and smashing good English china. Lamia was awake and had grabbed me by the curlies and spun me to the floor. She left me shivering one minute and boiling like a kettle the next. But worst of all, she filled me with discontent and a feeling that my life was insignificant and small. My 'content' turned into 'contempt' like soured milk. My safe and predictable life was now full of turmoil, and I felt utterly helpless as she started to peel me like an Onion, layer by layer until I cried all the unshed tears.

And yet, for all the havoc stirred up on the restless nights, I found I was feeling extremely creative, and new ideas would spawn from the empty void, and I felt a strong desire to express myself and uncover all my hidden talents.

My Pandora's Box was open, and I realised there were many gifts inside that hadn't even been opened. It was as if all my birthday presents were still left inside their paper wrappers and it was now time to rip them open. My life was definitely heading in a new direction.

Lamia had started a commotion, a recklessness that would take me on a journey seeking my inner truth and asking the unsolved questions of 'What is **Home**, what is **Love**, what is **Right Action**, and where are all the **Wisemen**?'

But Lamia wasn't here for a picnic, she wanted me to realise my own true worth. She shook me wide awake, and I could see the contempt I was feeling would suffocate me. I had to escape this miserable existence that was drying me out like a husk; it was time to take drastic action. It was time to peel my Onion, and I soon realised…

It was time to leave.

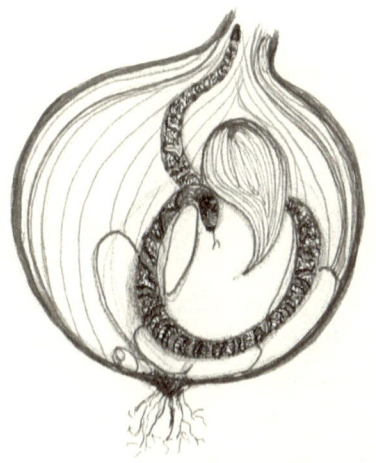

Night of Discontent

Hushed creeps the evening mist in subtle twilight
Birds herald home the newborn night
Veil the spider web in dewy silence
Uncoiling from her slumber, Lamia is awake

Virgin moon signals no danger and yet she stirs
Deep in her belly passion fires are lit, eyes open
Sharp breath intake, then deep exhale of emptied lungs
She sighs, as Earth moves another inch

It is time, the wheel turns and She is upright
Luna wings ride the night's dreaming claiming visions for her own
Pray you are safe from her vengeance, as men cry like babes tonight
Come quickly hide yourself under covers; Lamia is awake.

By Vivienne Mason

ONION GIRL

Dear Lamia

You are making me restless by keeping me awake, I only have a couple of hours left until morning and then I have to get up and brace myself for another busy day, dragging my carcass around from pillar to post. I am so tired and wish you would give me just a minutes' peace. I have taken to holding on to my rose quartz crystal in the hope it will soothe me and allow me to drift back to sleep. It is small comfort when you are so inconsiderate. Perhaps I need stronger medication as it is taking a while for HRT patches to kick in.

Instead, my mind has been mulling over the many vexations I have to bear, and you send me into a despair I cannot shake. I am surprised and shocked by what happened earlier today, or was it yesterday? You showed me the Key, the one you left in plain sight in the form of a beautiful man I was not expecting, and his sudden attention sent me on a high tide of awakened emotions. A rollercoaster ride, shaking me to the core. It has been so long since I have felt my heart race and a girlish flush across my cheeks. But yet there was a warning bell sounding that terrible pain always comes with wanting something you cannot have.

Is this the Key to my Pandora's Box, shall I open it now? Am I brave enough to face this mess I'm in? For I am so full of discontent it leaves a bitter taste. I embarrassed myself earlier with the Key and have been trying to find a way to make amends for my foolish actions. What was I thinking, and how am I ever going to look him in the face again? It was the worst kind of burning day, turning a beetroot red, comingled with embarrassment and the dreaded hot flush. Now I just want to forget it ever happened, crawl back into a hole as I slip into the shadows. I am so worn out with it all, and it seems I am totally unprepared for this 'meno' awakening.

I remain yours half-heartedly ~ Vivi ~

PEELING ONIONS

I lay awake clutching the heart-shaped rose quartz, my mind circling around like a vulture, looking for something to feed on and finally landing on the memory of Mother's Day. I started again to pick at the corpse of empty accolades of last Sunday. I had spent the day with the in-laws trying to feel included and hide my sense of not being appreciated as another Mother's Day goes by without a single gift. Gone are the days of innocent presents bought by the school committee with instructions to take five dollars to school to purchase that special gift for Mum. A little smile crept along my lips as I remembered the beautiful glass angels in tiny red boxes each of my sons had bought for me and were now collecting dust on top of the bedroom drawers. No wonder there were no gifts or specially cooked breakfasts. I had been acting like a banshee for months now and was being avoided. The punishment was I had to listen to my work girlfriends telling me tales of delight and surprise while accepting their beautiful handcrafted cards and gifts of fragrant body creams labelled as 'spa in a jar'. It made me feel nauseated, and then I realised it was now down to me to buy my own presents.

I turned over in bed and faced away from him snoring and thought of the Key and then quickly pushed the thought down below the tideline; it was not a good idea to dream those sort of dreams, but it would not die down. These newly awakened feelings of attractiveness and longing crept in on the silent waves and lulled me to sleep the last hours of the early morning.

Alarm bells sounding and the start of a new day so soon after drifting off, I let Ozzie get out of bed first while I cradle a hot cup of peppermint tea. I feel like I've been camping, sleeping on a rock, my head and shoulders aching after a night of bodily tension. Was it already morning? Then I remembered it was Friday, thank God I finally get a day off.

It was then on a whim I decided my Mother's Day gift would be 'not giving a crap today' and doing what I wanted. Sometime in the early hours I had awoken with the urge to write a letter. The apology to the Key and to try and make sense of what was happening to me. I read it now in the privacy of my bedroom and realised I must not send it as it was too provocative. It was just me behaving badly on another burning day - which was getting out of hand - and my irrational behaviour making me act very recklessly. What had gotten into me?

I saved the file under Lamia, for she was riding me around the paddock with careless abandon.

Dear Heart

Let me say first how truly sorry I am for my behaviour and I take full responsibility for all that happened that day. I feel so wretched and worn out with it all and humbly ask for your forgiveness. I did not mean to hijack you and rough you up in the way I did. It is unbearable for me now to think of and I have spent many hours ploughing over the scorched field while the storm still blew around me.

You asked me why I was red and couldn't look at you, it was a terrible moment for you to see me on a burning day and witness the fire's rage as it has been doing now for some months. I have tried to control it and failed, so have now asked doctor do-little for HRT exorcism which is patched in now.

Maybe in a week or so I will be drifting on a dead calm sea awaiting the mistral wind to blow me back on course for reconciliation. If you can find it in your heart to speak to me and allow a few more explanations and be it on a day when the wild horses aren't charging in the fields, then I can only hope that we come to an understanding. May that day be soon.

Onion Girl

PEELING ONIONS

I heard the boys leave for school a few minutes earlier and on that cue had gotten out of bed and now stood facing the pile of dishes in the kitchen, the ones that didn't make it into the dishwasher. Last night's meal left cementing on the plate and another day of house cleaning made its announcement. But it's Friday, my day off. I swore loudly and headed for the shower. For this was a no dish day, a grant a wish day, a couldn't give a crap day. A gift to myself Mother's Day, a grab your keys, you're leaving kinda day.

It didn't take long to sling a few essentials into my small suitcase; I had been thinking of catching up with my sister-in-law on the vineyard and now was a good day to head out to the country. I didn't even think of calling her first, I was so distracted and tired that I just got in the car and drove. It was becoming a regular occurrence too when I felt that the household chores were getting the better of me and I was failing at my motherhood duties, by neglecting them. I have always been tidy and like order around me but not anymore. I really couldn't find the energy to keep on top of it all and my own mess was creeping into all corners of the house. My floor-drobe clothing piles were tripping me over and I was behaving like the teenage boys I had given birth to. *Whatever!*

In the rush to get out the door I had forgotten to put another HRT patch on and was now driving on the highway out of Melbourne without a care in the world. Well I tried to convince myself that was the case, but it was so far from the truth. My head was a snowstorm, a whirlwind, a record on repeat. A voice screaming, a dull thudding, and a dangerous place for kids to play.

At 50 years old, I watched as my dreams turned into delusions, any aspirations smothered before the flames were big enough to burn bright. I felt the everyday closing in, mundane and mediocre, shopping aisles, cooking meals, housework, gardening, unending, never-diminishing responsibility of wife, mother, sister, daughter and friend. Sometimes the every day gets too much and I can't breathe. I needed space and time to be alone, to get away from it all. Not just a holiday, I needed a total change.

Whilst driving I thought of how I was feeling so average every day, I couldn't even drive the car into the countryside and think of one single thought that would make me happy or content. I had become boring, even to myself, a bland middle-aged woman with nothing witty to say about anything and anyone, especially myself. Triple F – fifty, fat and fucked.

I absentmindedly pulled at the thread from my top that had been tickling my hand. I had forgotten to cut it off and as my mind wandered to the dishes and the debris, and all that had made up my daily life in the weeks before. Somewhere along the highway I could feel the desire rising to simply drive into the traffic and it would all be over.

Where was my joie de vivre, my life vitality, my zest and vigour? I was deflating like a balloon and no one gave a crap. One thing that was growing by the day was my anger and frustration. Especially with Ozzie, my hus-banned, my betrothed, light of my life, boy of my dreams. My contempt was hard to hide now; we had reached rock bottom and my wifely charm was replaced with sarcasm and derision. I couldn't even blame Lamia for this state of affairs, or lack of. Life had become mediocre and predictable with him and I couldn't stand it anymore. But worst of all I too had become boring and it was hard to admit that I was the girl with the problem.

The road was becoming foggy just outside of Kilmore and I slowed down to concentrate. The hills were shrouded in mist and low visibility was making it hard to focus on the road. Then the car hit something out of the blue and gave me a jolt. Was it a tyre blowout or just a rock or did I hit a dead kangaroo? Not having any mechanical skills, I started to panic and ended up steering to the side of the road and to a standstill so I could get out of the car and take a look. It wasn't a good place to stop but I had no other choice. Soon another car was loudly honking its horn at me. I reeled off the usual expletives and hand gestures before checking out the car end to end. I couldn't see anything, no dents or flats, no blood on the bumper, but the hit had shaken me, and I just wanted to get back in the car and drive.

PEELING ONIONS

I must have been putting my foot down as I drove along the highway, for not long after I could hear a police siren and see the flashing blue lights approach out of the fog. My heart lurched into my mouth as I was already anxious, fraying at the edges, my stomach doing the usual somersaults. Once again, I pulled over and wound down the window. The fog was beginning to clear on the highway and the police officer stood at my car window.

'Do you know what speed you were doing just now madam?' He was keen to get his breathalyser out and ask me for my licence. I reached into my bag for my purse and gave him a guilty look. I wanted to explain that I was distracted but thought better of it and really, I didn't have a clue what speed I was doing. 'You were doing over 100 in a 90 zone and I am afraid I am going to give you a ticket, Ms Mason'. He used my name like I was a schoolgirl. It just made me so cross, but this was not the time to get all menopausal and mad. I felt like I should try to explain, but the strong arm of the law was making me nervous and all I could manage was a weak 'sorry I just wasn't thinking'. He got back in the police wagon and then took ages checking my licence. With his blue flashing lights, he sat smugly, writing out a ticket and fining me. All the while I sat seething as the thought of how my day had gone so quickly to shit. I should have stayed in bed, I should have stayed at home, I should have done those damn dishes!

I really did not want to have to admit to Ozzie that I had got another speeding ticket to add another black mark to my already stained character and more money to pay out. What the fuck. Just take a breath and suck it up princess, as I could feel the panic churning in my bowels. The thought crossed my mind that I could stroll out of my car, hammer on his window and demand the officer explain why he was making me wait so long for just a fucking ticket and if he wanted to arrest me and take me to the station then he better get some assistance as I was not going to go lightly.

Whilst the fog was clearing, the police officer handed me the fine and I watched as he drove slowly up the road and do a U-turn. Then an explosion went off in my head, I started to swear loudly and thump the steering wheel calling him all the names I could think of - 'dickhead, knob-sucker, bastard. How dare he!' I hollered to myself.

Turning the engine back on I copied his U-turn and headed for home. This time driving very slowly to the annoyance of other drivers as I cursed myself for getting a speeding ticket and paying into the Police Benevolent Fund. I imagined the smug look on his face as he got to fine another sucker like me.

I seethed all the way home and boiled my way back into the driveway. If I wasn't going to drive the car without getting a ticket, then I wasn't going to drive the car at all. Irrational thoughts followed me back into the kitchen and instead of putting the kettle on and making a cup of tea, I headed downstairs to get my passport. My temper tantrum was waiting to erupt like a volcano as I slammed a few more clothes into the suitcase and took one last look at the unmade beds of this morning. Both sons left their rooms in a shemozzle and the crumpled bedsheets reminded me that I needed to put fresh ones on. Bugger that, today was going to be such a good day and now I am pissed off at myself yet again. My day off, and I so wanted to feel the wind in my hair. It was blasphemy to have to put up with this. Can't even get in the car and go for a drive without the day turning into a bloody battle.

Instead I pinned the fine to the fridge and put some lipstick on, brushed my hair again and grabbed my raincoat, before quickly pulling at the thread once more, this time snapping it clean off. The bus would be by in a few minutes and I was going somewhere, as anywhere was better than here.

On the way to the airport, my mood lightened. It seemed an age since last night and the morning drama. I had forgotten deliberately about the apology letter sitting in my laptop but now my thoughts were drawn back to the Key. What if I did leave Ozzie and found someone else? What would happen if I started dating again? What if I lost weight and turned myself into a drop-dead diva? What would happen to the boys?

PEELING ONIONS

No use thinking about what-ifs. I tried to think of home; where was home, why did I feel so alone and what had happened to me, turning 50? I suppose I could start playing a violin but that's not my style as I hate feeling sorry for myself more than anything. What would happen if I left home and never came back? It was worth a try to see if they would actually miss me.

CHAPTER 2

Peeling My Skin
'ONION GIRL SPEAKS'

Transitions, the ones we make every day whilst moving from place to place, job to job, task to task. The small insignificant steps we make when getting in the car to drive to work and navigate through the rush hour traffic. The mind is on the road, the taillights of other cars, we drive with one foot riding the brake pedal, watching the mirrors. Listen to music and sometimes sing along badly. Then getting out of the car, we arrive at the office, move to the desk, sit and admire the paperwork scattered, small notes left by anonymous visitors, instructions, and cries of help. Turn computer on, log in, move to the kitchen, make a cuppa, say hi to the work colleagues and sit down to tackle the daily grind. Then later leaving work, we drive again home, in more heavy traffic and we are tired, the day is long. Getting home, walk in the door, shoes off, bag down and face the kitchen, wondering what on earth to cook for the family. The time in transition feels wasted, in no man's land not really feeling anything. Not concentrating on the movements of the body or the mind. A limbo. We may even eat our food without tasting or talk without listening.

These small transitions from place to place, task to task, while we are unaware of our body and our emotions, could be a good time to check in, see if we are okay, ask if we are settled. Deep breaths, relax and unwind and tune in. Make an effort to be mindful, alert instead of being on autopilot. You may have missed that small detail of the dog or cat lovingly greeting you at the door. The birds singing in the trees and the sun shining. You may have forgotten to appreciate the day, the sky is blue, and the clouds are fluffy, the flowers are in bloom.

Unobservant. You feel you are just getting from place to place, doing whatever it takes to get through the day and safely home again, looking forward to a good night's sleep.

But say this never happens, sleep evades you, the tasks are never-ending, the work is increasing, and the daily traffic heavy. Your family have their own demands, with cries of 'what's for tea Mum?' and the answer is getting harder and harder. Every transition is an ordeal, your feet are no longer skipping down the pavement, but trudging along, dragging your heels. You may have to speed up rushing into people, as time slips away and you are now running late, there are deadlines to meet, people you must see. From pillar to post you are pushed and squeezed, prodded and poked. And all the while your mind is busy, it flits like a bee from thought to thought, buzzing along the chore list, processing tasks, planning and mapping out. You may be playing a certain thought over and over, that bad outcome, ill-spoken word, that insult. And while you are at it, think of all the other insults and mishaps you are dealing with. The music is getting loud and you want to scream. The boss has been hovering at your desk heckling you for some results you don't have. Your friends are too busy to see you, your children want you to drive them everywhere, and your partner, well they have their own shit too. Dumping it on you after every day, giving you the rundown of what's been happening in their life. The woes and torments they are putting up with and grinding you down with the whole sorry story, day after day. It is impossible to escape. You have offered a kind ear for years now, but they are unaware you have your own shit story too and haven't got the energy or the will to regurgitate it over again.

PEELING MY SKIN

This picture I paint is what it has been like for me. I call it 'threshold syndrome', when walking through another doorway, I have to wear a different hat, a work hat, mother hat, or social butterfly hat. The act of moving from place to place gets harder and I feel uncomfortable in these rooms, I want to be invisible, unseen and unheard. Inside the office I crave the sunny day, with the gentle buzz of insects and birds as company, the sky above and the freedom of the open road.

I want to walk along the river, the peace and tranquillity of water. A scene to drink in and paint. Get creative. Express my inner voice and calm down. Relax, breathe in and out, meditate and let go of all encumbrances and start my day with the intention of living my life for myself, as I want to, on my terms. The art of allowance and acceptance flowing through my body and feeling that transition, notice the steps as I walk over the thresholds, concentrate on the time it takes to walk to the kitchen and put the kettle on. Or strolling along the river and enjoying the small breeze on my face and warmth on my skin. These little thresholds crossed are there to be savoured. Our life is short, and many hours are wasted not noticing how much enjoyment there can be in the very minute things.

But time slips away from beneath our feet and soon we will have to move on, but hopefully not before we achieve our lifetime goals and discover what gifts we have been bestowed with. This precious time to be with our loved ones and cherish ourselves and others. Find a home, love with all our hearts, practice what is right and just be kind to others, seek out wisdom. The precious commodities of existence are essential along the path of our life journey. And if we are lucky enough to have gifts that we remember to unwrap then you may also experience true contentment. Cup full.

I am Onion Girl, I have lived a life, unseen and unheard. I do not venture outside. I am snug and comfortable inside my onion, building layers around me, year by year. I don't want to be disturbed; my life is a simple one. I protect myself from hurt and rejection. I bolster myself against criticism and am an expert at spotting well-meaning words wrapped in empty sentiments. I don't want to be in the limelight or be famous in any way. I'm not interested in money, wealth or status. I just want to stay deep inside my Onion.

My tough outer skin is my protection. You can try to cut me, but your knife may slip into your finger. And when you peel me, only to discover yet another skin layer wrapped even tighter than the rest. My flesh is smelly; you can't slice me without crying. And when you do get through there is another surprise; I am actually quite nice and I taste amazing, especially when cooked with bacon. I tantalise the tastebuds and bring hungry hoards to the kitchen.

But don't bite into me raw, I will leave a bad smell on your breath to be avoided. For onions don't like being manhandled, oh no. We feel so much better when we are planted in the damp earth that covers our bodies, we can send our green shoots out towards the sky and a beautiful ball-shaped flower will bloom white or purple. We have seeds that scatter, and these precious black spores hold the source of our nature.

It feels safe, mostly but lately my outer layer has been peeled and ripped in places. I even have a small desire to explore outside the onion, get out there and see the world. I notice this when I am lying awake at night and there is a ringing in my ears and a buzzing in my belly. Perhaps I could venture out and make a few friends. Say hi to people, see if they notice me and my creations. I am curious. I want to know what makes people tick. How do they manage out there in the big wide world, playing their guitars and painting brightly coloured canvases? I long to write songs and sing in front of people. I want my paintings hung high in the halls. My poems whispered on lovers' lips and to feel proud of my achievements. I have few aspirations but lately something is moving from deep within and I cannot push it away any longer.

These feelings are new to me and I can even pinpoint the day when I felt the itch.

PEELING MY SKIN

It was on the long walk by the Yarra River, when the sun beat down on the pathway and my feet crushed the gravel making dust trails as I wandered by. My thoughts scattered by the orchards and fried under the drifting clouds. This quiet day was a time to sit and contemplate, to meditate by the bubbling brook. The sounds of rainbow lorikeets screeching ahead alongside the cries of cockatoos. I sat down and drank deep glugs of water on this hot, dry January day. I had taken to outdoor meditation to cast out the thoughts of the everyday, and to calm the horses. For I had noticed they were charging about the paddocks these days, their thundering hooves getting louder.

I sat awhile as it was exhausting trying to walk in 37 degrees; not a great time to be outside in the hot dry Australian summer and murder if you haven't got a hat on. Lucky for me I wore a large brimmed hat and a good pair of sunnies to boot. And in the quiet still air I went into a slumber.

CHAPTER 3

Peeling Flesh
'ONION GIRL BREAKS FREE'

Peaceful silence, wind brushes, a gentle breeze sways the branches. I try to grasp the silence in my own thoughts, the gap between the mind's eye and the actual stillness within; it is mostly impossible. I am not used to it; you say you strive for peace to be unobserved and distant. This is new to me. I am retreating into myself. Silence befalls me like a death in the family. It is a stranger's embrace. In the breathing space, I am surprised to find a glimpse of happiness, a self-contentment. Is it real or imagined? Breathe deep, let go. I wave my little white flag to you. My need for peace leads me to the void, on the edge, my true self is revealed. What is it to be alone? My life lived for me. Quietly, contemplative, reflective and hushed. Thoughts bubble up, bird song permeates, sun shines, blue skies, no plans. Just a day of rest. Heartbeat, lungs full, tide out, solitude. Distant from loved ones, revelations of need. Time flows and I jump into the river, going with the flow – take me home.

I sat in meditation by the Yarra riverbank, and in this daydream, I went down a stairway and into a room of marble white, where I saw two chairs, one for me, the other for Onion Girl. Here we sat in *the great light. Large spheres placed in our laps, changing colours of green, red, blue, indigo and pink. Our thoughts dissolved, we tuned in and when all the rainbow colours had circled about our beings, one white light shone deep within, and the globes glowed gold. Now the vision came. My older self, Mason sat opposite Onion Girl; she is the protector. Her hands reached across to say 'I am here, don't stress. You are stronger than you think, and it is time to come out from the Onion. I will be here always, my arms around your shoulders. Vivi you need to be brave and step out into the sunlight. It is time to let Mason go into retirement. She needs to rest. Take the wheel Vivi it is your turn to drive. Take heart, Mother is here always'.*

With that I awoke and now understood to complete the journey, it is time to expand. Let go of all things and embrace the Universe. It is always constant and true. Trust in opportunities and doorways become openings to explore. This transition is easy!

PEELING FLESH

Dear Lamia

I know I have placated you with my recklessness and flown the nest; how proud you must be seeing me take action and not just sat snivelling on the sofa wondering why my life is looking like a bowl of cold porridge with the spoon stuck in. No bear would want to eat it now!

Yes, it did feel good to do something wild and unpredictable and I know you are laughing at me, tossing your head back and screeching into the wind. You're uncoiling in me now and I feel you slither around my stomach bringing the heat to my skin. Let the burning begin of my old life, it lays before me and I am full of contempt for my paltry efforts at trying to make a comfy home in Melbourne. I need more than this. Where is the passion, I hear you whisper, your cutting-edge ideas, the gifts you are hiding or worse, simply ignoring? It is time to strip off the old skins, they are smothering me and now I can't breathe under all these Onion layers.

The sweat is moist on my face and I feel like I am bleeding from my eyes, for you want blood, sweat and tears to show I am feeling your claws pinch at my soul.

Come wake up Vivi, you are not dead yet. Far from it.

I lay on the airport floor gazing out at the blackness of the evening, shining lights reflecting off the runway. Flights came in and out and I had found a quiet spot to stretch my legs and rest my weary head on my one item of luggage. It had been relatively easy, getting to Tullamarine and going to the Singapore airline ticket counter. I asked for the next flight to London and said my mother was gravely ill and so the counter staff managed to book me onto the 4pm flight to Singapore with a two-hour layover before climbing aboard the flight again to Heathrow.

I used my pink debit card, which was full of our savings and spent more than I would like to admit on a return ticket to London. Getting on board was easy and it really took no time at all as I had slept the whole way from Melbourne. Now I was in the airport zone C with the shops and the busy travellers buying duty frees. I had eaten little on the flight and managed to get some McDonalds just moments before. I turned on my phone to check messages. Why was I feeling so blasé about it all? I had just left my family, my home and my job out of the blue and flown seven hours, running away like the wayward wife and mother that I was. The trip so far was a lot easier than driving to the vineyard, along that foggy road, with that surly copper stopping me in my tracks (although he was only doing his duty), as I drove recklessly along the misty highway. Now it turns out that this cop, in doing his U-turn, had changed the course of my life and as I remembered his car cruising like a predator off down the highway, that feeling in my stomach squirmed as Lamia was now on the rampage.

By now Ozzie would have come home from work and seen the speeding ticket on the fridge. The boys would have eaten pot noodles and gone to their rooms to play computer games and Ozzie would have gone out on Friday night to meet up with his 'old man' friends, as our sons called them. He would have barely missed me and if he noticed the car, would have automatically assumed I had gone out with a girlfriend.

My phone bleeped the various messages and then I saw it. One message from my younger son, then two, bleep bleep. In total there were 21 messages.

'Mum can you pick me up. Mum I need you, please I want you to pick me up,' and so it went on.

'Mum, where are you? Forget it, I got the bus. Any chance you can take me to a friend's house? Mum please. Please. Please.'

And on the messages went from my second son Robbie, who was 14 and had a lot of Year 9 friends and parties to go to. He was turning into a social butterfly and wanted to be out and about, trying his luck at heading into the city and staying up late. I lost count the number of times I ferried him around. It's what we mother's do isn't it? My stomach churned and I felt I was never going to be able to explain why I had suddenly left without warning. Do I text him back and say, 'sorry darling I am in Singapore, on my way to London'? It sounded so surreal. And yet the enormity of it didn't affect me at all. I was going away, that was it. I may return when I was ready, but stiff shit. Derr! Whatever.

The next leg of my journey, for 13 hours I watched movies and listened to music. I ate the crappy flight food and thought to myself it was too late to turn back anyhow. So what if I had suddenly left them? Did I feel guilty? Nah. My mind turned to the sunny summer days that were waiting for me in Devon, my mother's cottage, the warm bed, and open windows, with a breeze rustling the curtains. The open fields of swaying grass and hills all green and full of goodness. The river winding down to the sea and the ocean blue. My home.

The transition from Melbourne to London had been easy, but now I was at the front of the queue in passport control and this sour-faced woman looked at me and then my EU Passport and said it was out of date, which I knew already and offered her my Aussie one. She was not happy that I was in this queue of EU and British Nationals, as my passport had run out nine months ago and I should have joined the queue for Other Nationalities. Like hell I will.

I was now tired and feeling stroppy and my nose was getting out of joint. How dare she suggest I join the longest queue in the history of airport queues, when I was a British Citizen and if the passport office thought it was good enough to issue me one at birth then it was good enough now, out of date or not. The particular rising tone in my voice was not too helpful and the sour look on her face said it all. 'Stand over there and I will get my supervisor'. An older Scottish man came over and asked more questions, like why I am here, for how long and what was my occupation. I answered dryly and he then said I had an attitude. Lamia wanted to strike him in the face. He chastised me and said I had to fill out an immigration form and then he let me through, not before saying I should renew my passport in future. Fucking idiot, my own country won't even let me in without all this bullshit. I stomped off with my case on wheels and made it through customs and to the bus station in terminal two. It was 6:30am. 24 hours ago I was in Melbourne and now I was in London.

I breathed in the air and choked on the diesel fumes. Bought my bus ticket to get me to Woking train station and then the best train in the world, takes me all the way through the countryside, skipping through the counties, Hampshire where I grew up, Wiltshire, Somerset and finally Devon. I am from Wessex and this is my home. Put the kettle on Mum.

Should I ring my sister?

It was not unusual for me to just turn up, I never announced any of my visits to Mum as she would plan an entire banquet for my arrival and stress over the clean sheets and dust on the curtains. She was now getting too old for all the shenanigans of playing hostess and her anxiety levels went sky high if she knew any of her children were flying. It was much better to just enter the back door and with a cheery 'hi there'. I had her door key with me always, it was my lucky charm and came with me wherever I went. It meant that I was never locked out of the last English home I ever had. It was my security, my talisman and now I was going to actually use it.

The train sped along the countryside, with views of the cows on the ancient farmlands. Station by station getting me closer to my destination. I finally relented and gave my sister Biddy a call. 'Hello, it's me, guess what, I'm on the train to Axminster, do you think you could pick me up?' Her sweet voice trilled with excitement and I managed to leak a tear or two before brushing them off. 'Yes, of course, what time do you arrive? Why didn't you tell me you were coming? Mum is going to be so happy'. Wow I hadn't had that reception in a long

PEELING FLESH

time, and it was a shot in the arm, the spiritual lift I needed to feel wanted and appreciated. The dam walls nearly busted then but I held my tears back and gazed out the window.

Counting down the stations and finally the train pulled in and I got out further down the platform than expected. I could not see my sister anywhere, but then she walked out through the doors and saw me immediately. It was like a movie; we ran towards each other and embraced, while other passengers looked on or simply ignored our un-English style of greeting. We hugged and jumped about with excitement. Triumphant I had finally made it home. I could kiss the ground. It didn't take long before she asked what was going on and I brushed it off saying I needed to come and see you all and get my Devon fix. It was a simple enough explanation and I wasn't challenged. But I knew there would come a time when I would have to spill the beans and admit that I had been very unhappy, and I was finding things hard to handle with Ozzie and the boys. But for now, we got into her little car and drove through the Devon sunken lanes, with the familiar high hedgerows and at the break-neck speed all UK drivers seem to go, we careered over the bumps and around the bends. If a tractor was coming the other way, then we would brake suddenly and make a speedy reversal up the road to a layby.

Just as I was holding onto my seatbelt, the sea view came around the corner and I was captivated by its beauty. Biddy was telling me about her job and how she had to make an excuse to come and get me, as Saturday mornings she worked in the local art gallery and had closed the shop. But I didn't care, she was here, I was here, and all the world was a sunny Devon day. I wanted to shout out the window 'the cream teas are on me'!

The back door was open, and Mother's cottage looked a perfect haven; the small kitchen with ancient cupboards and drawers led into the lounge room which was unusually spacious. The large stone fireplace made a perfect winter centrepiece and Mother was sitting in her recliner chair with the usual rollers in her hair. Her face lit up when

Biddy called in from the kitchen and she leapt out of the chair when she saw me too.

We hugged, kissed and laughed and then Mother took my face in her hands and looked straight into my eyes, giving me the health check scan, and I knew she could see my pain. 'Vivi what are you doing here, is everything all right? How are the boys? Was your flight ok? Wee, I'm so pleased to see you. Put the kettle on Biddy. Where are all your bags? I've got a casserole in the oven'. Just like Mum to have everything ready for me. My heart sank as she asked me about the boys and the tears in my eyes told her far too much already. Luckily Biddy distracted her with bustling in the kitchen asking where the good cups were kept.

I sat down and took off my shoes and, in my dad's, old chair, drank in the cottage décor. The pictures, photos and paintings; some I had done. My grandmother's teapots, the orange sofa, our dad's table, it was all so familiar, and the fireplace was ready as always to be lit.

Mum was chatting on about the weather and the buses and the village people walking their dogs and how we were to leave the back door open to keep the fresh air coming in. Mother nattered on around us making a beautiful fuss and filling my heart with love and warmth. It had been over two years since I'd seen her, and we were both excited and I can tell she cannot wait to hear all my news.

She looks older since I last saw her, but she seems in good health. She walks now with a stick and tells me how life sucks when you get to old age. She wishes she could get back out more on the buses, but she is finding it hard sitting around the bus stops and generally the drivers don't help you with the shopping like they used to, but coming back from Seaton the other day, a lovely man carried her bags to the back door for her.

I am tired and probably jet-lagged but as it is lunchtime Mum insists that we sit down and eat her beef casserole and she could pop some peas in the microwave if we like. In no time I am sitting around the dining table, Mum eats her meals on a tray on her lap, but I am facing my sister tucking into good old English food and it feels so good to be back. I am not ready to tell them about the brick in my stomach every time I think of the boys as the guilty feelings are beginning to sink in.

On the way up the stairs Mother is telling me my room is ready, the same as ever and that she likes to keep it that way just in case I come and now it is perfect timing. It is called the poppy room; I have red pillowcases and different red shades of cushions and lovely fake poppies in a vase. She is very proud of it and I am not about to criticise it in any way. My bed looks so cosy and I open my window out into the farm lane with views of the old farmhouse opposite. We are in rural Devon, the cows moo and there are chickens clucking in next door's garden. Mum tells me the cockerel calls every 30 seconds and that the admiral who lives across the street has been complaining, but it never bothers her, she loves the sounds of the country and he can cock-a-doodle-do it all day long.

Dumping my bag and laying on the bed I say I would like just a little sleep before I come downstairs again. This is my excuse as I want to cry, and I cannot hold it in anymore. And I don't want to shock them with an emotional outburst that is so unlike me. But first a shower, the perfect disguise for a crying baby and so I gather fresh towels from the linen cupboard with the expressed instructions to use the white ones as Mother always uses the pink or yellow, but don't use the blue ones as these are for visitors! I laugh to myself as my mother is a great old gal and staying with her in Stanley Cottage is going to be interesting.

Sometime later I come downstairs and Biddy has gone home to her own cottage in the next village. Mum has the TV up loud and I call down to greet her. I put the kettle on again and we sit for hours and talk about the family, nothing heavy just going over the boys, their health, school, my work and Ozzie's job. She quickly turns the subject to the village, her hobbies, how much wool she needs at the next shopping trip and if we are going to Tesco supermarket could we get her some more paracetamol as she is about to run out.

It is here in the lounge room that I feel the old Vivi reappear, with talk of wool and arts and crafts I can feel the urge to make a new basket and give it to Mum as a gift. I am beginning to unwind and although the fog of jet lag is still in my head and behind my eyes the tears still unshed, I want to dance around the room and be a young girl again. Take away the burden of parenting, it is my time to be mothered.

I think of my bike in the shed which will probably need its tyres pumped up and my wellington boots just in case I am walking in the muddy lanes. It is nice to hear that everything remains as ever, as Mum hasn't thrown out a thing, I have coats and shoes and undies. By now I have discovered that I have forgotten to put undies in my bag and of course, this sends mother into conniptions. 'What you have come all this way without knickers! You can try some of mine, but they will look like bloomers on you'. First thing Monday morning we would get on the bus and head into Axminster to get some. As it was Saturday night, mother headed to bed with her usual port and brandy and I stayed downstairs in the cottage with just a side light on.

The cottage is 17th Century and full of character. It has wooden beams across the white ceiling a lovely old feature and the stone fireplace has remnants of black soot from decades ago. The walls are thick to keep the heat in and cold out and the windows are small. The roof would have been thatched in the old days, but now it has slate tiles. It was once the old post office but the two cottages were knocked into one sometime in the last 50 years and so the kitchen is down a step and has an older feel, with a bathroom leading off this. And like all English cottages, our neighbours are right next door, in the attached buildings. In the dark the cottage looms with shadows and the clocks tick. Mother loves to watch the time and so there are two clocks in the lounge room and one in the kitchen. They all tick at different seconds and you cannot escape the time, which is set at least five minutes faster in each. The kitchen clock is the only correct clock and reads 9:30 pm; it is now 6:30 am Sunday morning and Ozzie will be asleep in bed.

PEELING FLESH

I wonder what he has been up to this weekend and whether or not I should call him and explain. I don't feel I want to, but with common decency it would be better to call him and get it over and done with. I look at Mum's phone and my own telephone number is written on the pad in big felt tip pen so Mother can read without her glasses. But I can't be arsed; I really don't want to talk to him. Perhaps in a day or two when he has figured it out that I fled the nest and he can feel abandoned by his wayward wife.

My bedroom at night takes on a whole new persona, no longer is it a cheerful cottage bedroom, but a creepy old gloomy room, it is completely black as I enter, with no lights up the stairs and no lights in the village, apart from the moon. My curtain blows in the breeze and I fumble for the bedside lamp. I can hear the owls high-pitched calling from the hay barn and there is a chill in the air. I don't like my room, it gives off shadows and the black night air is thick, it gives me the shivers. I am a grown woman but the bedroom at night is always a challenge. But tonight, I decide I must just sleep and get into the new time zone by going for a country walk first thing in the morning.

I toss and turn and am still awake at 3:00 am. I thought I had closed the window, but the net curtains are blowing in and out. The sounds from outside must have woken me and I can hear a fox making a cackling noise. I am unaccustomed to the sounds as it is hard to place where they are coming from. I stumble to the loo and find the light switch, trying not to wake up Mother, who I can hear snoring from her room down the hallway. Perhaps it is just my paranoia, but I thought I heard a creaking on the stairway. This is not the first time the cottage has disturbed me, and I am not sure it likes that I am here. I make my way down the stairwell, and as they are very steep, I hang onto both bannisters, unlatching the old wooden door to the lounge room I fumble for the light switch again. The TV is on.

I find the remote and turn it off then get a glass of water from the kitchen. Maybe it is just me, but I feel like I am being watched. Just to clarify things, I didn't grow up in the cottage, Mum moved here when Dad died and has been here for 20 years. We have been visiting her since before I had the boys and after. Biddy moved down from her flat in London when she had her son and lives in the next village. We are 'grockles,' outsiders; we are not true Devon folk. I think the cottage is trying to tell me this and I slink back up the stairs to my room and keep the bedside light on and sleep for another hour until daybreak.

I had forgotten that the dawn chorus starts at 4:00am, the blackbirds sing, and the sparrows chirp, and all the world is awake to the sound of birds preening their feathers. The cockerel is awake too. There is scratching in the ceiling and on the rooftop. I try to stay in my bed a bit longer, but it is no use. I head to Mother's room instead.

She is lying on the far side of her bed and I creep in next to her. The feel of her warmth is so inviting, and she turns to me and says hello. I snuggle down under the sheets and she gives me the hug that I am in need of. The journey home has been a long one.

CHAPTER 4

Peeling Soul

'MOTHERHOOD CALLING'

My dear darling son (no.2)

You have been the 'light of my life' since I felt the very first kick inside my belly. I have delighted in all that you have done since the day you were born, from mimicking dangerous dinosaurs in our garden to the many hours spent drawing sharks and playing with the trains on the floor. As you have now grown up to be a fine young man, I can only see a fantastic future ahead of you and am so proud of all that you are now and all that you will become.

My love is strong for you and is a never-ending source of abundance from which there is no end. Each day I count my blessings that you are with us, and both me and your dad have given you all we have.

But there is a time when you discover that your parents are human beings too, we suffer the same trials and tribulations that everyone else does, we are growing up ourselves through life experiences and *sometimes we are not equipped with the right tools and demands of modern parenting.*

I am truly sorry that I am not there for you today on your big day, it fills me with shame, and I have spent the night worrying about how you will go with your mock exams. It is out of my hands darling; I cannot come back just now.

My own life has been a challenge lately and like all relationships, there can be conflict, and your dad and I have needed to sit in separate rooms. We just don't seem to have the warm empathy that couples have these days, and our constant bickering has left me feeling frayed at the edges. Please don't blame Dad for my leaving, he does his best and is under a lot of pressure at work. I have a great respect and love for him as he has been the best father to you boys, it would be unfair of me to berate him now.

I know you are angry at me and that I cannot change. Please try to find it in your heart to speak to me again, we were always such good buddies, you and me, and I love our closeness. I am spending some time with Granny and your Aunt Biddy and I know you think I have gone away on holiday without you and in many ways I have. But it is to give myself some time out, take stock of my life and recharge my batteries.

My anger and frustration was beginning to take its toll on you all and it is not fair of me to pretend otherwise. This is called menopause darling and all women go through it, but it comes at a time when you boys are teenagers and therefore the hormones in the house have escalated to the rooftops.

I will keep writing to you since you will not answer my messages and hopefully, I will get you on the phone so I can hear your gorgeous voice.

Yours truly, ever-loving and caring, constantly worrying, sorry I have been a letdown,

Mother xx

PEELING SOUL

It's now been a few days since leaving Melbourne and I have arrived to perfect sunshine and the glorious lush green fields. Every shrub has burst into abundance after months of rain. I have walked along the country lanes with hedgerows towering above me. Stinging nettles two metres high and the rich honeysuckle perfume fills the air while bumblebees cruise along the laneways.

Each morning I set off on an 8km walk and breathe in the fresh farm atmosphere and the smell of silage reaches my nostrils. Finally, I am getting my fix of England. The village has plenty of rolling hills and views of the River Axe and out to sea. Every now and then I have to stop at the farm gates to catch my breath and to feast my eyes on the valley. It is simply amazing, and Mother is saying how I have bought the Australian sunshine early to her wet and soggy shores.

I put my old guitar into repairs and booked my first lesson with a guy who has the longest dreadlocks. Mum and I wandered the market stalls, buying underwear and fresh fruit and veg, locally grown. We had lunch and I drank cranberry cider followed by parsnip, apricot and walnut cake – *ooh err.*

I re-learnt the hedgerow bird names on discovering that I no longer knew them after being away for many years. I asked Mother what sort of bird was making that happy trilling noise. It seems I had forgotten the sound of a wren. There are also robins and a family of blue tits, not to mention the chaffinches and siskins in the bush outside the back door. You can't go anywhere with Mother without getting a history lesson, she is the expert on architecture, she is a natural tour guide and can tell you anything and everything there is to know about Devon village life. Only my mum has a full-size cut-out of Nelson in the laundry room for Trafalgar day, it nearly scared me to death when I saw this uniformed man lurking behind the washing basket.

On our first bus trip I sat next to a lady who said she had been saving the seat for me. She asked if I was spiritual and told me she was a highly sought after medium. We exchanged phone numbers and we had a good yarn. Seems I am on the right path already, she told me she had Romany blood and I was going to Spain in July for a big event. Fancy that, me going to Spain.

It feels like I have already eaten far too much from feasting in the pubs, to buying our groceries at the local farm shop which has a fantastic array of fresh produce just begging to be made into a yummy dish. I spent an evening with my nephew at the local fish and chip shop down by the sea, in a fishing village called Beer. They served the largest cod and chips I have ever seen. The fish was draped over the edges of the oval plate as it was so big. The chips came separately, and he scoffed the lot. Me and Biddy had a small portion each and it was the best I had ever eaten. I was getting fatter by the day.

On our first Sunday, Biddy and I walked to the next village of Musbury, who were holding an open garden fete. We explored the lovely walled gardens and thatched cottages with their veggie patches and vast herbaceous borders. One particular house meandered up the hillside with secret pockets of lush flowers and huge oak trees. But then by chance through the thicket we saw the neighbour's massive derelict and overgrown house with bow-fronted windows. It looked impressive and would have been a grand house in its heyday. We asked the village postmaster who had lived there, and he said it was owned by a mad old lady who had moved out years ago. National Trust had tried to get her to do the repairs, but sadly this grand house had gone into ruin. It was once a posh hotel and even had apartments. But now it was hidden by brambles. A perfect setting for an Agatha Christie novel or a place for Lamia to haunt. I wanted to go and explore the hidden mansion, be a daredevil and sneak through the fence and take a proper look around. Typical of England to have this grand folly obscured amidst the overgrown weeds.

The most perfect thatched cottage in the village was serving cream teas in the garden which featured a quaint bridge across a trickling stream, beautiful rose bushes perfumed the air and closely clipped borders made this the quintessential Devon chocolate box setting.

We sat out on the terrace eating scones with homemade strawberry jam and clotted cream on floral plates and drinking out of fine china.

The days were already whizzing by and my life was one glorious romp through the open meadows. I was exploring the hidden country lanes and walking across the cornfields, getting lost, listening to the tractors in the distance as I lay in the grass hidden from view. It was on these days that I shed my tightened outer skins and dreamt of what my life would be like if I were to be very brave, go off on an adventure and not let Lamia stomp on my daisies.

One day soon after I arrived, I returned from a walk and Mother's eyes were on me. 'Why haven't you called Ozzie, you know you can use the phone, is there something wrong?' I knew she had been digging for information and I was trying not to give too much away, but sooner or later I would have to confess to having come here at a moments' notice. Would she understand me and how I had been feeling? I was so engrossed in living like a teenager again that I was forgetting I was a mother and wife. I had responsibilities and duties to perform, and both were seriously lacking. I didn't even feel guilty that I had left without a word and was rather happy in my new carefree life; after all, I told myself I deserved it. I had earned long service leave from my marriage and wanted my freedom. Lamia was smirking to herself when I thought like this.

I sat in Dad's chair and offered to make the tea. 'It's not been easy lately, Mum.' Now if I am going to talk to Mother, I have to get comfortable as I know she will interrupt and it's hard not to get frustrated and cross with her. I don't need Lamia for this as she naturally always brings out the worst in me in these situations and I have never liked to be questioned and being put on the spot.

I could hear her from the kitchen saying, 'It's none of my business what you do, only I have noticed you haven't really mentioned Ozzie and the boys, and it's been nearly a week now. I'm not going to pry into your business, but you seem to be a bit off'. Mother could spot a lie, so it was no use giving her a false story, she was far too astute for that. She also knew me very well and could probably tell that I was not being fully upfront with her about why I had come to visit. 'Don't get me wrong, Vivi it is absolutely lovely having you here, and you certainly brought the good weather, but sometimes you seem a little distant, is everything all right?

We sat with our mugs of tea, and I began with a very weak excuse, 'I was feeling home-sick, I needed to come and see you and get my fix of Devon country air. I've been feeling restless, and lately, the thought of you sitting here in your cottage makes me want to jump on a plane, I just wanted to see how you are'. This wasn't entirely untrue, I did miss England, the rolling hills, the cliffs and the sea, its history, and Mother was getting older and I never knew entirely how much time we had left together. It broke my heart to think one day she would not be in her cottage, sitting with her crochet on her knee, watching the village go by with their dogs and nattering to me. I loved her stories too; her rich history of life, and her knowledge was incredible. I never really liked school and could ask Mother anything and she would give me my lessons on history and geography; whatever the question she would have the answer. Even now her love of books filled the many shelves and coloured every corner with portraits of Vermeer on the wall and of course, my dad's aircraft.

Here in the cottage Mother lives a genteel life. The local bus stops right outside the door, she can explore the towns far and wide with ease. Although lately she was finding getting on the buses harder and she was loath to use her stick, but there was no denying she was getting old. Thoughts had crossed my mind that I should stay and look after her, be the dutiful daughter and perhaps help her around the house, clean the kitchen and declutter the drawers. But the mere mention of me cleaning up anything was met with hostility as this was seen as an insult to her housekeeping skills and she was not an old cauliflower head yet.

PEELING SOUL

We sat and cosied up in our chairs and I listened to her while I sipped my tea and asked her, 'What was it like for you during menopause? Did you have any symptoms?'

'Well if I did, I can't remember; I was working in the Pathology lab at the time and my boss was a bit of a bastard.' I loved it when mother swore; she would colour her language every so often and make her tales amusing. 'He would never have known I was going through menopause as I was determined not to show it to anyone, no one wants to know when a woman is going through the time of life and the hot sweats were the only symptoms I had. It was not that bad, actually. I know some women go through hell and your dad would not have put up with a neurotic female in the house, so I kept it all to myself. Your dad couldn't stand neurotic women.'

So, there I had it, Mum didn't have many symptoms and if she did, she was not going to divulge them, and she hid them from Dad. Well, that puts me in my place as I am feeling very neurotic every day, and I can relate to being a mad woman doing psychotic things, acting recklessly and wandering around talking to myself. This conversation was not going well, as I knew she would not be happy if I told her I had just suddenly left my home in Melbourne in a tantrum, recklessly driving down the highway, getting a speeding ticket before jumping on a plane. So, I shelved the conversation and steered it around to common ground and our favourite topic - cooking.

I watched her sip her tea, pulling a slight grimace, and wondered if I had put her sweeteners in. After a while, she sighed and said, 'this is always your home Vivi, but the boys need you and you should be there, with them. I don't need you to come here and check up on me, I am fine, I love my cottage and I am very comfortable here, I am not unwell other than old age and it is entirely normal for me to feel the aches and pains of my generation, but I am not in need of you coming here every year to see if I am all right.'

So, she thought I was checking up on her! I didn't know whether to say more or less about it, but there was no doubt she was getting older, and could probably do with a bit of help around the house. I had many phone conversations with Biddy about how mother was coping and if we should hire home help, but when we bought this up with her, she was adamant that she did not want someone coming in and cleaning using bleach and moving her belongings. And I knew that we would not be able to persuade her otherwise.

Mother was not even keen on me opening the lounge room curtains a bit further to let in more light, as this meant the whole village could see her sitting in her chair, so I closed them back to where they were. A few days before we had an argument as I wanted to wash the chair covers, as they were in a neglected state, but I was told the cat liked to sleep on the chairs, so there was no need to remove them. I lost my cool as the cat was long dead and had ripped them off and thrown them in the bin. Mother was not amused and swore at me from the kitchen saying it was her house and how would I like it if she came to my house and rearranged the furniture. But at least we could now sit in the old Parker Knoll chairs without the nylon scratching my legs and I was happy.

I felt entirely at home in the cottage with Mother, we shared many interests like art and crafts, and I was beginning to fantasise about getting a job here. It was entirely feasible. I had been looking through the papers and found plenty of part-time jobs in the local pubs as it was the summer holiday season and most restaurants and bars hired seasonal staff. I could even work in an office as I had plenty of experience and getting around wasn't so bad, although I didn't have a car, I could use public transport. Recently there was a job advertised for a marketing assistant at the local cider factory. It seemed my ideal job was right here in the village and I could walk to work. It was perfect as I loved cider and all the other wines made on the premises. This was certainly an option, to get a local job and live here for a while until I sorted myself out.

I was not sure if I should mention this to mother as she was not keen on having long term visitors, but it planted a seed in my head, and I was starting to fantasise about living in Devon again. I had a long-held dream that I would buy a cottage nestled in the green fields, close to the sea so I could sit on the beach and watch the waves coming in, be near the fields and laneways for my long walks through the ancient woodlands.

Years ago, I had tried to persuade Ozzie that we should move to Devon to be near my mum and sister, but he wouldn't even think about it. He said there was no work for him and that it was not a good idea. I tried for years to change his mind as the boys were younger then, and my own sister was a single mother and could do with the help of a close family network. But this dream never came to fruition. But now here I was with all these new possibilities ahead of me, I could get a job, live here in the village and do whatever I liked. This new-found freedom was quite exciting, and it gave me a certain spark I had not felt in a long time.

I had been living in Australia for over 13 years now, but still it didn't feel like my home. I could make a new home here and come back to my roots.

Mother started to talk about the boys, and I knew I had to ring Ozzie. I had been putting it off, but the feeling of guilt was creeping in. I told mother Ozzie was working and that I would try to ring him in the morning when he gets home. She seemed happy with that, and by then she had changed the subject to the school kids on the bus swearing at her and last week a tramp in the churchyard had told her to *'piss off you old cow'*. 'I was going to offer him money, but he was very rude, it's a shame what the world is coming to these days, and in the churchyard.'

I laughed to myself with the image of my mother taking umbrage at a vagrant swearing at her in her straw hat and red shoes. She would have been very put out. But yes, it was time to ring Ozzie and the boys and find out if they were missing me. In my quiet village, time was running out and I had to face the music. I hadn't even thought about my job in Melbourne either. Now there was a problem!

CHAPTER 5
Peeling Responsibility
'WAYWARD WIFE'

Dear Hus-banned

I have tried to call you but there never seems to be anyone answering the phone. By now you will have guessed that I am in Devon with Mum and that everything is okay with her. She has not had another life-threatening event but is rather well as it happens.

I know I should have told you where I was going before I left, but I didn't feel that I needed to. You have been so wrapped up with the auditors at work these days; it seems I can never catch you at a good time to tell you anything.

Our darling son Robbie would have got his letter by now too, so I am guessing he told you of my whereabouts and that I am taking a break. As we don't seem to be communicating very well at the best of times, I am resorting to old-fashioned snail mail.

Just to confirm if you are wondering, I will be away until I feel like coming back. This means you and the boys will have to cope without me. I cannot totally justify why I am saying this, but you are difficult to live with and I don't feel you support me. It is a one-way street. You come home, your tea is cooked, you have the luxury of sleeping in the chair, and for that matter all night too. While I lay awake wanting so much more in my life and feeling like I am doing everything and getting nothing in return. Don't I deserve to get a little bit more than just you snoring next to me?

I have worked for years now, from when the boys were little, and I have decided it is time I took long service leave from you all.

Please tell the Top Bloke to get a temp in to do my job.

And by the way, there is my speeding ticket on the fridge for you to pay.

If you could give me a call when you are free or send me an email, I would love to hear about the boys. Our son had his mock exams this week and I wanted to know how he went.

And if anyone asks, just say I have gone walkabout, as a wayward wife and mother.

Yours disrespectfully

~ Vivi ~

Biddy and I have been sitting at night playing our guitars and talking about the old days. It has been such a relief to talk frankly with her about my present circumstances and come clean as to why I left the boys. She wasn't totally surprised to learn I had just jumped on a plane and was very supportive. We spoke each night of our love lives, or the lack of romance, and we played guitar until our fingers ached. We ate

PEELING RESPONSIBILITY

dinner late, as we wanted to take an evening stroll before we sat down to the table, and life was going at a comfortable pace. We would head off up her street, which had two pubs at either end, and walk towards the river and hang over the bridge watching the large fish in the reeds. Then around the town streets with the cobbled pathways, we would do a circle, perhaps stopping at the village store to buy a few bits for dinner, including a couple of bottles of wine, or sometimes cider.

I loved the summer nights when we would take our drinks to the garden and sit watching the sun slowly set behind the church spire. The bells rang out loudly every hour and when it got dark, which was after 10:30pm, we would stargaze.

It was here I poured my heart out; about how I was feeling like I didn't want to be a mother anymore, and that being married was such an ordeal. It was nearly 25 years; a life sentence and one should be able to take a break after that long. I acknowledged I was changing, growing out of my old self and into the new. I wasn't sure I wanted Ozzie in my life anymore and was certainly not a very good mother. It was all too much for me, living a predictable life and feeling the drudgery day after day. I needed to feel free again.

The jungle drums had also sounded around the village, as Mum had told the people at the bus stop that I had arrived out of the blue just to surprise her and how happy she was to see me walk through the door. Even my own friends back in Melbourne were asking me where I was. Ozzie had obviously told them that I had gone away, and I had received a few emails from the girls at work asking when I was coming back.

But to be honest, I didn't care what was happening in Melbourne, I was embracing my new life in England and was planning my trip to visit a close friend in Scotland. I even had the offer from my cousin to travel to Europe with her in a few weeks' time. Life was so full of sunny days and starry nights and I really didn't want to think about the boys or anything else back home. So, I didn't. When we had finished our nightly chats, Biddy would drive me back to Mum's cottage where I would ask her to leave the car headlights on while I made my way into the gloom. The cottage was pitch black, the village was in darkness apart from the night sky and I needed to navigate through the kitchen to find the light switch before heading upstairs.

Mother was in bed by the time I got back and the atmosphere in my bedroom was always one of eerie disquiet when I entered it late. I found this unnerving and each night was an ordeal as it was getting harder and harder to sleep in my bed without having to leave the lights on. I always felt this presence watching me and Lamia was smouldering under my skin. I was becoming paranoid about the ghost and had even talked to Biddy about it. There seems to be a blackness about my room that I don't like. I wake up sometimes and have to switch the light on. It's as if someone is in the room with me. I don't like it. Perhaps Lamia is making me paranoid.

Years ago, Ozzie had gone to sleep for an afternoon's kip after a big lunch and came downstairs asking if anyone had been up sitting on the bed. We all looked at each other, wondering what he was talking about. I had long suspected there was a presence in the house, but not where Mum lived. She mostly occupied the bedroom in the newer part of the cottage, so any ghostly spirit had left her alone. But lately I was not feeling so welcome in the bedroom and lay awake listening for sounds and looking at the shadows. I was becoming restless.

Lamia symptoms seemed to be more apparent when alone at night with time to think. It was then that I noticed I had been scratching my skin throughout the day and that my hair was getting unruly, curlier and dry. At least I wasn't spitting obscenities at people, like I was during my working day, and I had mastered my frustration with action. When I wanted to walk around the fields, I could let off steam and Lamia was calmed by activity and not sitting still. At night the scorn and bile that ran through my veins would surface and I knew I was in for a temperamental stormy sleep.

PEELING RESPONSIBILITY

You need a loverman, she would say. You need to feel his touch and get lost in his passionate embrace. You need to be free to do what you want and not answer to anyone. You need me to shake you up and get your blood moving. You need to feel alive. You have not been honest with yourself, or true. You deceived yourself with promises of completion but now you know, nothing is ever complete. You have to keep moving and evolving. It is time to expand and grow outside the Onion, shed those skins that have been strangling you. Let me help you with a knife.

My Darling Sister Blister

I have been thinking of you lately and was so surprised to see your email. Yes, I am well and enjoying my Summer in Devon, where it hasn't rained for weeks now and I have been keeping myself fit gadding about the countryside, and today I spent walking the cliff tops and stuffing my face with Cornish pasties and Devon ice cream.

I know you have seen Ozzie and you tell me he looks a little dishevelled. Not sure why he is letting himself go, as he won't answer my calls. Thank you for your kind words of love and support, it has been weeks since we last saw each other and I am happy to learn of your new job.

My job is on hold, or rather they have got a temp in to take over until I get back. I have taken unpaid leave and so have found it rather hard on the purse strings. You sound so concerned for my wellbeing, and there is no need to be. I am happy here staying with my mum and sister, it has been a real pleasure seeing them again, and having the newfound freedom of doing what I like when I like, and I know you will appreciate that I needed the rest.

We have shared many stories about what it is to feel love and be loved, which are two different things and I guess I haven't felt loved for a long time. I know you say this is silly, but it's true. My family, I love without question, but I don't seem to be appreciated like you are. Like I said to you before I left, not one Mother's Day card or present. And this leaves me feeling dejected. I have worked for years slogging my guts out and now I am taking time off, it is my Mother's Day present to myself.

You always said be kind to yourself and I guess I am learning to do this, as for years I have berated myself for being fat and overweight. You know I have been struggling lately, as I have told you many times on our walks along the Yarra. Ozzie has been so distant; he doesn't even know I am in the next room. He just sits at the dining table night after night painting his miniature soldiers and I don't see him. At night he snores, and I want to stab him. I feel like he left the marriage before I did, so no, I do not feel guilty.

Don't worry; I have plans to go to Scotland on my next trip and enjoy my time exploring Europe and beyond. Who knows I may even get a job and live in the village, as the mad cat lady! Perhaps you would like to come and visit me for a well-earned cream tea as they have amazing scones at the farm shop, and I am discovering my love of gin. The local cider factory has been making it for weeks now and I am enjoying the tangy taste with tonic and a slice of cucumber. Biddy and I are planning a night in the meadow behind Mum's cottage which hasn't been cut for hay yet. The grass is long, and you can see the whole valley. We will sneak up there on Summer Solstice night to watch the sun go down whilst drinking our scrumpy – oo err.

Yes, I will keep in touch and I do appreciate your letter. I am totally fine, honestly, and I would never have been able to get through the past six months without you.

Yours waywardly ~ Vivi ~

PEELING RESPONSIBILITY

It was clear to me by now I had stripped myself of responsibility of motherhood and wifely duties. I did not think about them and I tried to imagine my life in England. The first peeling of the onion was done. I also had no job and no income so began to think of ways I could travel to see my friends. My cousin had been in touch saying she was about to go to France and Spain and if I wanted to come with her, I was welcome to do so. But first I had to visit my hometown, the house where me and Ozzie lived when the boys were little. Our first house we had bought together and poured all our dreams into, the place I had left all those years ago. I still had friends I could stay with and it was all arranged I would get the train to Alton in Hampshire and stay a couple of nights before heading up to Scotland. It was years since I had been back to my old stomping ground and the train ride went quickly.

I was met by John, my old work buddy, and he drove me along the familiar country roads to Alton. We had lived in this old market town in Hampshire for over 10 years and I had given birth to my boys at the nearby hospitals in Basingstoke and Winchester. I was a Hampshire wench by birth, and I savoured the sights as we sped along the byways into this quaint, but slightly shabby historic town.

The first thing I did after dropping my bag off was walk into town and towards the bank. We had opened bank accounts for the boys when they were little, so my name was still on the statements. Both boys had accumulated a small amount of money from the savings we had given them for birthdays and Christmas; it was supposed to be their small nest egg for when they grew up and wanted to travel or buy a car. And I was thinking I should close the accounts down and transfer it to my own bank account which I still had open. There was enough money in both accounts to keep me going for a few months at least and it seemed to be the perfect solution. Apart from the fact that technically it wasn't my money.

I walked into the familiar bank and the teller asked for my driving license. Again, this was out of date. She told me I needed better proof, and so I handed her my Australian passport, and my out of date UK one. She frowned again and I told her I had ordered a new UK passport and it was in the post. It took a very long 10 minutes to get her to agree to give me all the money from both bank accounts in cash. But she did, and now I had enough money to last me. I walked into my own bank a few doors down and deposited it, ordered a new cash card and left enough money in my purse to last the week. I felt so free.

I knew Ozzie would not be impressed that I had pilfered the boy's bank accounts and that I would have to pay the money back in time, so I made a note of the amounts in my diary and went about looking for some new clothes. The summer sales were on and I needed to freshen up my scant wardrobe. Buying new clothes was exactly what I needed, and I even took time to get a leg wax and my nails done. Whatever should I do next?

Later that night I met up with my old workmates in the Eight Bells Pub and we drank far too much and sang a few songs. My old boss even offered me my old job back as secretary to him and it was fairly tempting. The town was so bright with bunting flags adorning the shopfronts and people spilling out onto the streets from the pubs, a real English summer, everyone happy and in good spirits. I felt truly welcome back into my old hometown.

The next day I stood before my old house, its wrought-iron gate and picket fence. The beautiful cherry blossom tree had grown larger and filled the garden. It wept over the circular brick paving we had placed around it. The hedge adjoining the neighbour had also become too big and in need of cutting back and the orange blossom tree was now several feet high. This home was a haven in the days when the boys were little and they played in the back garden. The curtains remained the same and the front door had been painted red. But still, it was recognisable and felt like I could just walk right in. I had dreamt of coming back here and setting up home again, but always the house was empty with some belongings stored in boxes; there was no furniture and nowhere to sleep. I also dreamt that I still owned this house and it sat waiting for me to return and I would one day be moving back in. Now I stood as if a stranger and was too shy to knock on the door to see if the people who bought it 13 years ago were still here.

I walked around to the backyard, which had a large wooden gate onto the road behind. It was still familiar with a new and much bigger shed, but that didn't take away the old feelings that I had of the boys peddling up the pathway on their tricycles. Their joyful screams were encapsulated in the photos I had of them. Their little bodies bathing in the blow-up paddling pool and taking naughty boy pisses into the bushes. It was a lovely place to bring up a family, but sadly it never felt like a home. But at least it held some outstanding memories of my boys and their early childhood and the many BBQs we held with friends and family. I smiled as I recalled the firework nights on November 5th that lit up the frosty night sky and the time a stray rocket went speeding off and landed under our old Volvo car before exploding. I sighed to myself and thought of the happy days.

My own childhood home in Farnborough, I refused to return to as this held painful memories of my father and the many arguments we had. I had left home at 17 years old to escape his tyranny and did not have the urge to return there in the slightest. Since he died and Mum left for a new life in Devon I was quite content to believe that we had all made a new home with her too.

But the reality was I had never really lived in Devon and sometimes I was still the outsider. Having never put down any roots there, I was an annual visitor like the swallows that soared up and down the road looking for insects. I made my temporary nest in the bedroom above the kitchen and tried to feel like I belonged.

Perhaps moving to Melbourne was a good idea at the time, having spent many years trying to get Ozzie to agree to relocate to Devon. It was my second choice to go to Australia and make a go of it, for the sake of the boys, to give them a good education and to give Ozzie time to spend with his ageing parents. His own father had died a few years ago now. At least he did get to spend some precious nights with his father, at the weekly Thursday night dinner with his family, and routine we have kept up for years.

When we first arrived in Australia, we moved in with his parents and before long rented the green painted weatherboard house opposite. I soon got a job with a tax agent as office manager and started to make friends, and eventually we bought a house in Eltham and set ourselves up in a nice suburban home with a pool. Generally, life was good in this leafy suburb with the gorgeous smell of gum trees, screeching parrots and nearby schools, even a train link to the city provided all my family needs.

It was all supposed to be going so well, but Ozzie didn't get the job he wanted and instead worked at a lesser role for lesser wages. He was unhappy and I tried to compensate.

My home was no longer a haven to me, but a chore to maintain, dust and hoover. I had become staff, the unpaid worker. It was a burden and needed constant attention. And then lately when I became perimenopausal, I started to neglect it. Lamia was becoming active by the day and she hated any cleaning and sometimes would smash the plates to avoid washing then again.

But the question that remained unanswered was did I ever have a home where I felt I belonged? A peaceful haven for me to be alone and content in. I asked myself this before I left and now facing my old house in Alton, I knew in my heart that I had never really felt like I had a home spiritually or physically. It was as if all the homes I had ever been in were temporary, no fixed abode.

What is this feeling of home? Where do I belong? These questions nagged at me in the undercurrent of my emotions and the stirring that was occurring with Lamia at night. The bedroom disturbing my dreams and Lamia lurking in the shadows as if mocking me and saying, 'don't get too comfortable, you will not be here for long. She doesn't want you here; you don't belong anymore'.

PEELING RESPONSIBILITY

It was true, I could pretend all I wanted that I could pick up my old life, take up my old job and move back to Hampshire. I even toyed with the idea of working a summer job down at the beach, in a café. I was being lulled by the English summer days and long nights, the buzz of insects and the call of the crickets. It was beautiful, every day gorgeous and sunny, all the old houses looked cute in their ancient rows, and people were friendly, chatting to me on the train and at bus stops, in the shops and supermarkets. My old friends glad to see me and the pubs a real delight with drinking, singing and beer. I was gorging myself on all my old favourites; cider, gin and real ale, cheese and onion crisps and the odd cake here and there.

I spent a day at my favourite town of Winchester, strolling around the Cathedral looking at all the graffiti carved by the choir boys in the 900 years or more of its existence. The tombs of kings and bishops, the monuments to our rich past, and the library of chained books full of the calligraphy Mother loved. She had even exhibited one of the manuscript pieces here on the 900 year anniversary. It won an award. I loved the market and was free to walk around the old Great Hall, with the round table of King Arthur hanging high on the wall. It didn't matter to me that this was not the 'real' one, but at least it gave all visitors a sense of the magical place an old country has. Maybe I was home in those moments, being a tourist, a voyeur, travelling around with my backpack, so maybe the sense of freedom was my home and haven. It was unclear to me, but it felt good to be away from the daily grind.

I left Alton with a case of South African wine John had bought for me saying it was as good as Australian wine any day and so I lugged it back to Devon on the train, looking out the window and dreaming of the next part of my adventure, Scotland.

ONION GIRL

Dearest Sister Blister

It is so easy to get swept away with the sunny day, blue sky and fluffy clouds. A visit to my old hometown of Alton to see it all again, a real treat as I love the old high street, the shops and many pubs. Even my old bank manager welcomed me, and I told them I was thinking of moving back. Well, I needed new bank cards!

I stayed with friends and took an evening stroll to Chawton to take photos of the house of Jane Austen. The village is celebrating Regency Week and Alton has events and costume plays being held in the Memorial Hall. Bunting and banners deck the high street and it looks so pretty to be here at night before all the tourists get a chance to ruin the ambience.

I have been shopping and discovered my old favourite store, Peacocks. Bargains galore and I bought t-shirts, a pair of shorts and a couple of cotton blouses. I couldn't help noticing the 'bar staff required' notice in the Wheatsheaf pub window. My school friend Diane came to visit me here one night and we sat outside in the market square drinking cider and catching up on old times. She told me about the new man in her life and we had a few laughs until late. I have known Diane since I was 16. She is as crazy as ever, bubbly, bright and up for a good laugh. She wants me to come and stay for the weekend on my next visit.

The next day I got on a double-decker bus to Winchester, my favourite Cathedral town, driving through Old Alresford and Kingsworthy. I was trying to take photos and video the road as we raced along.

Winchester city is so old, the buildings still as I remember. The Cathedral had loads of school kids being ushered in for the school year-end services. I tagged along with them and didn't pay the entrance fee. I am still staggered by the architecture, old tombs and carvings, and went to see the famous Winchester bible for Mum, which is held in the chained library. I asked the attendant if I could climb the stairs

PEELING RESPONSIBILITY

to the upper galleries where all the old statues from Roman remains are held and the ring collection stolen from the bishops' tombs. There is even an old glass jar holding St Swithin's heart. Quite bizarre.

When the sound of the organ filled the halls, everyone stopped to listen and the choir held our hearts in our hands as we traversed to the rooftops with their sensational sound, and for a moment we were set among the angels.

It's just as well I am doing a lot of walking as I couldn't resist buying from an old delicatessen some blue vein cheese, seed crackers and lush English strawberries washed down with a local cider. I sat by the river and let the sound of the water soothe my aching legs. Then I set off to explore the Great Hall, with the table of King Arthur. It is not the real one, but it draws the crowds and if you want, you can dress up in the fancy dress to have your photo taken.

I sound like such a tourist and I just wanted you to know that I am really having a good time. Each day is a new beginning for me, and I am living in the moment. I don't have any plans and am just going with the flow. You said I would miss my family and I do, but they are not on my mind at the moment. After spending years with them being my main priority, this time is for me. You asked me if it was right to just leave them and not take them with me. Well, I have to say I do struggle with my own conscience at the thought of me leaving as I did, but it is a small pain in comparison to the overwhelming pain I have been suffering lately. That lizard brain of mine saying I am not good enough, not working hard enough, not earning enough and not finishing all my art projects. It is guilt that has been slaying me by day and suffocating me by night. What about me, what about my mum and sister, don't they deserve to see me and spend time with me? After all, that is all we have - time.

Right action is not always putting everyone first; sometimes, we have to do things for ourselves, to survive, to revive. Find that essential part again. I have tried to do the right thing for years and got nowhere. I know you say it is selfish of me to be gadding around the countryside, without my boys. But that is it; they would never come with me anyway.

For years I have wanted to go out and explore the world, travel and have holidays, but Ozzie would never take time off work and said school was more important for the boys. Not even during their school holidays. He worked and I picked up the pieces, coming home at lunchtime to feed them sausage rolls and sandwiches. I never quite got away from all the chores, and I do not feel guilty about leaving them. Ozzie is a good father and he can look after them well enough, and let's not forget they can all feed themselves, they are practically grown men.

I went to visit our old home yesterday and past memories returned of when the boys were little. It was good to see it but also my heart did not want to admit that the time lived there was also sad. My dad died when I was in that house and my life changed forever. I could never get Ozzie to move to Devon to support my mum and sister and therefore we left them when we came to Australia. This has been a massive part of my guilt for a long time.

You must try to understand what I took away from them when I left. All possibilities of seeing the boys grow up, of birthdays, anniversaries and Christmas. I stole all the small pleasures of visits to Granny's house and playing with their cousins. I did not know what I was doing and was blinded by the idea of a new beginning. It was not the one I wanted, but the second choice and I worked hard to put our lovely home in Alton on the market. This is exactly the reason why I should have taken the boys with me, I hear you say. Well I didn't. Perhaps I will pay for it in the long run.

My mum is well, but she is getting old, and there are times when I think I should move back in to be with her and spend the last years of her life making sure she has everything she needs. But sadly, for me, my family have grown away from me and do not warm to me moving in with them again.

PEELING RESPONSIBILITY

I say these things to you as I know you will understand. It has been hard lately, and the burden of motherhood has taken its toll. I do not feel that I owe Ozzie anything, I have given my life for him, given up all that I have for him and now you want me to come back because he looks like he has joined Al Qaeda with his grey beard and unbrushed hair. Well, it's a shame that no one noticed my own fraying around the edges as then we wouldn't be here.

Perhaps it is too late for me to go back anyway now as I am cleaning out all my old beliefs and cannot find the Wiseman I have been looking for! As the longer I live with men, the less I understand them, they are so different from women. It's hard to believe we are even compatible as when it comes down to it, they are all just a bunch of pricks.

I don't want to come home until I understand what love is, what home feels like and what is the right action. I have been wrestling with these issues on a daily basis and cannot find the answers.

You have been such a constant friend, and I know you are concerned for us all. But let me do it my way and if I stuff it all up, then that's my problem.

I thank you from the bottom of my heart for being the close sister I longed for when the nights have been dark, and I share your compassion. In no way do I want to hurt Ozzie or the boys, but it's me who is drowning. I threw myself the lifeline when I left three weeks ago.

I know you will check in on the boys for me. I thank you for that. I will always be grateful to you my sister-friend.

Yours truly

~ Vivi ~

Biddy was waiting for me at the station, all smiles and hugs, her long hair gleaming in the sunlight. It made my heart sing, for we had been close sisters for many years now, although during our teenage-hood we fought like cats. But we shared so many memories of our dad, who was not an easy man to love by any standards and Mum was always making excuses for him and we never really knew if he loved us.

We got in her small car and sped away, heading for the beach and the promise of a day under the cliff tops on the pebble beach at Seaton. It was her day off and she was keen to go and do something, so we planned to sunbathe on the deckchairs and have lunch in the Chine Café on the seafront. It was good to be back in Devon and the familiar views of the River Axe winding down to the coast was as picturesque as ever. Often, we would walk along Seaton seafront and watch the visitors eating their ice creams. It was great for people watching as no one cared if they were fat or thin, people bared their fair skin no matter what during the English summer, even if it meant getting burnt. This was so frowned upon in Australia and I was taken aback from the blatant sun baking with skin cancer being a major scare around the globe.

We envied the families who had hired their beach huts as they had the added shelter of an umbrella and the easy life of putting the kettle on just when it suited them. A family sat eating egg mayonnaise sandwiches, another Cornish pasties and chips. It was great to see the bucket and spades and blow-up floating toys, not to mention the noisy kids and their constant need for attention.

We settled down on the beach with the backdrop of the red and white cliffs, for this was not called the Jurassic Coast for nothing. Fossil hunters had been coming to these cliff walls for years on the hunt for ichthyosaurus bones and trilobites' shells. When the boys were younger, we took them out with digging tools so they could excavate the walls themselves. It was fun but Mother always warned us of the dangers of rock falls.

PEELING RESPONSIBILITY

But on this day, it seemed so perfect and I was enjoying my homemade cheese straws and egg and bacon quiche, washed down with rhubarb and ginger cordial. I loved the farm-cooked produce, it was so wholesome, and Biddy had been eyeing off the lemon tarts.

We decided it was too good to waste the day, so we stripped off and bathed in our undies, the icy waves making us screech with laughter and the sharp stones under our feet unbalancing us with every step. Next time we would bring our bathers and sea shoes.

I let the waves wash over me and saw that Biddy was still standing waist-high in the water, clenching her teeth and making funny noises as the incoming waves lapped at her bare waist. She watched me swim out, calling for her to just get it over with. The freezing cold soon ebbed away, and I was baptised in the English Channel. I floated on the tide, relaxed and soaking up the endless horizon, drifting. It was a glorious feeling to just go with the flow each day.

The afternoon went quickly and soon we were back in Biddy's cottage with our wet hair and undies hanging out on the line. We made a cup of tea and thought we should really check in on Mother and take her some fish and chips for tea.

I was headed to Scotland the next day and had to get up early, get on a plane from Exeter to Inverness and I needed to pack a few things before I left.

Mum was sitting in her armchair on our arrival and although she no longer eats a big dinner at night, we know she can never resist a fresh piece of battered cod, and we all sat down and scoffed the lot. To walk off our feast, we headed to the river to watch the silver mullet swim amongst the river weeds. It was always lovely to be in the village and although there was no longer a pub to drink in there was still plenty of things to do especially if you liked walking.

ONION GIRL

The river wound its way down to the coastline, and the white swans nested in the wetland estuary. I never got tired of this landscape with the ancient hill fort of Musbury watching over us, being the one landmark that made this green land so unique.

It was getting late and Biddy headed back home, leaving me to clear up the dishes. Mum had gone to bed and I was tidying up the place when I spotted a photo of all our boys together. It had been turned away from view for some reason. They were aged eight, seven and five; my boys with Biddy's, such little buggers Mother would say. And in that instant, my heart sank. How much I missed them when they were this age. So uncomplicated and fun.

I decided it was time to try and ring them again to see if they would talk to me and for me to hear their voices. I was in need of their company, I wanted to hug them and say I'm sorry for not being a good mother and say I'm sorry I left you as I did.

CHAPTER 6

Peeling Regret

'MOTHERHOOD LOST'

The phone rang and rang until eventually, someone picked up the receiver. There was silence on the other end, and I said, 'Hello it's me'. Still more silence.

'How are you, what have you been doing?' I sounded so lame and then eventually the male voice said, 'Nothing much, just watching TV.' It was now time to work out which boy I had on the phone as they both sounded the same. So, I asked, 'Is Dad home?'

'No, he hasn't come home from work yet'. It was 10:30am in the morning here in the cottage and so 7:30pm Melbourne time. I'd had a bad night thinking about them and what I was going to say. I had been calling for a few hours now with no one picking up; I was getting frustrated. Finally, one of my sons was on the other end of the line and I struggled to find something to say.

'Has he been working late? What time is it there?'

'When are you coming home?' Son No.1 who had answered the phone said, with a certain directness I wasn't expecting. He was 16 years old, and very much the passionate supporter of all things Dad.

'Well darling, I am not sure at the moment, I am going to Scotland in a few hours and I wanted to see how you all are.'

'You could have told us you were going.'

'I didn't really know I was going myself; it sort of just happened. Please don't be cross with me darling; I am trying to work things out. Is Dad all right?'

'He's fine I guess; we don't see him much, but you could ask him yourself if you wanted to.'

'I have darling, I have tried to call him a few times, written to him too. Did you get my letter?'

'Yes.'

'I tried to explain things; I'm taking a sabbatical visiting Granny and doing a bit of travelling.'

'You are not the only one who needs a sabbatical, what about Dad?' Son No.1 was sounding gruff and accusing. I could feel the tension and sadness in his voice, and it cut me to the core.

Just then he handed the phone over to Son No.2 and I started the same conversation again.

But it felt hopeless, the boys did not want to talk to me, they couldn't find the right words and nor could I. It was difficult to tell what they were feeling, and the conversation lay stagnant in the water and a silence crept over me.

PEELING REGRET

I had nothing more to say to them other than I love you and see you soon, which felt like a lie, an empty sentiment, as I wasn't planning on coming home yet, but it just came out naturally.

What was becoming of me and my relationship with the boys? Had I lost them when I lost myself? Could they ever understand what it was like for me, being the only female in an all-male house? They didn't even understand their own feelings; I was asking too much of them and they were bewildered.

At least Robbie had sounded more convincing and I loved that he spoke about the cat which had taken to sleeping on his bed. A small consolation for a young man, I guess.

It depressed me that I couldn't hug them and kiss them and let them know it would all be okay. I needed to feel them like when they were little, give them kisses and cuddles up on the couch. Gone were those days of simple mothering pleasures, as the lads started to grow beards and soon, they would become men. Did they still have the same feelings towards me?

I doubted it. I doubted everything; I was lost to myself and to them. The brick sunk deeper into my belly and I cried to myself in the bedroom. Motherhood gone.

I suppose the only consolation I had was I had enjoyed every minute of being their mother, making models out of cardboard, swimming in the pool, cooking their favourite meals and taking them out on adventures. The time it took to raise them was over in a flash and the precious moments of mother and son were memories for me now. Was that it? I couldn't believe it was over.

Perhaps if I spoke to Ozzie, I could get a better idea of what was happening at home, see if they were eating well and remembering to lock the doors. I could tell by the cold reception it was not going to be easy getting back into their good books.

I was a failed parent, an absentee mother - mothers never leave their kids, no matter what. I had told myself that they no longer needed me; they were grown up and should be exposed to fending for themselves more. Doing their own washing and making their beds. What sort of parent didn't give their kids responsibility? You needed real-life skills if you were going to survive in the big wide world.

But for all the justification, there was no getting away from it. I had left them and from all accounts, Ozzie was taking it badly. He had let himself go and had been seen in the garden, looking unkempt like a hobo with a shaggy beard and dark, sad eyes. He was not being the super Dad that I had envisaged him to be. Was it all my fault that being left as a single parent would be the straw that broke the camel's back? Or could he do it alone? He seemed so underwhelmed by my presence every day; perhaps this was a cruel kind of wake-up call for him. But it had not been a bed of roses for me living there either.

I wanted my mother to put her arms around me and tell me it was all going to be okay, but then I would have to confess to my sins of being an absentee parent. I should have known to trust her more, as she came in the bedroom and she sat on my bed questioning my face, the tears still damp on my cheeks, and those beautiful steel blue eyes scanning for a reaction, assessing the damage, peering into my soul.

Ozzie had rung her a few days ago and she wanted me to know before I got on a plane to Scotland. She had spoken to him for a few hours and started to tell me how he was the best guy she had ever met, such a kind gentleman; I should not take him for granted.

And I never thought I would feel it, but in that instance, I had to agree with her.

PEELING REGRET

Dear Darling Son No.1

My instincts of motherhood kicked in when you were born as I knew the moment I met you I was in love and to see your dad's face beaming with such excitement was elating. And not a moment has gone by without you filling us with pride, especially when we watch you play in the school band.

Your true talents are yet to unfold, and I know that life will give you many challenges, much like the one that you are faced with today, knowing that your mother has chosen to be so far away from you.

This leaves you feeling frustrated and abandoned by me and I am so sorry darling, but believe me, I do understand what it is like to be put in a position that is not of your doing and being forced to make adjustments to your life to accommodate the actions of others.

Please find a little sympathy for me as I am struggling at the moment and want to say the right things to you but don't seem to be able to find the right words.

I love you with all my heart and would be there in a heartbeat if it wasn't for the fact that I have been struggling with myself and menopause.

I would like to hear all your news about your latest concert and how well you all played. So, if you want to drop me an email that would be great.

Love and hugs

Mother x

Scotland

I don't know if it was the Highlands, the lochs or the empty beaches that filled me with the desire to lose myself in Scotland, the mountains with their evocative names towering into the blue sky, and the long sandy beaches that stretched for miles in both directions. Meandering amongst the rocks and the pools, I truly felt I had escaped my suburban life and had been transported to a new land, and it felt wholesome. A feast of much-needed nutrients fuelled by the clean Scottish air.

My long-time friend Sandy and her husband welcomed me into their home, and we walked the dogs on the beaches near Elgin and Inverness and they took time away from their lives to show me the Highlands where the colours of the lochs and mountains fed my artist spirit with new ideas, absorbing into my veins. I really felt I could disappear and never be seen again. It was vast and moody, the mists rolling in from the seas, each mountain had its own climate, the glorious sun shone through reflecting on the deep lochs and valleys, purple hews, blue and green painting a palate on my imagination. We walked through the forests drove for hours to the west coast, and ate mussels, fish, fresh scones and jam. I had never tasted such gorgeous food; it was as if every bite was a new experience, a delicious morsel, and I feasted my eyes and my belly. There was nothing I could not see that didn't fill me with awe, I was in love with this place.

The days went quickly, and it was here that I saw my first pod of porpoises, skimming the waves in Moray Firth. My first taste of Highland seafood was Cullen skink, smoked to perfection, and the whisky was light on the tongue but did a Highland jig in your throat and burst onto your tastebuds. I even loved the ruined churches, the remains of the castles, and the history whispered in my ear. This is what it could be like if I left and came to live in Scotland. I could do it; I actually felt that this land was calling me to act.

So, the seeds were planted, and I began looking for adventure. Why not spend some time away? I had not planned to leave and work overseas,

PEELING REGRET

but the temptation was so thrilling. Just get a job and move. My heart was saddened by the loss of the boys and their smiling faces, so I tried to bring some sense into my head. But the universe was showing me all the open doors; Devon where Mum lived had jobs for me, my cider factory admin role had been advertised in the local paper and was waiting for me to apply, even my ex-boss in Hampshire had offered me my old job back and even now Scotland was calling me to take a massive leap and lose myself in the Highlands.

I put my toe in the North Sea and waded up to my knees. It was chilling to the bone, but I loved it. How anyone would swim in this sea was beyond me and even though this was summer, my bare legs were red with the cold for over two hours afterwards. It was seriously chilly, and winter here would be a challenge for only the brave hearts of the world.

I had never seen so many coats hanging in the hallway. All different thicknesses and waterproof lengths. Ones for a light drizzle and thicker more robust coats to keep out the cold chill of a stout Highland breeze, and then the heavy trench coats for the winter snow. This was serious outdoor clobber and my trainers did not last too long in the dewy grasses of the forest floor. We walked for miles looking for geocaches, the hidden treasures placed by fellow Cache enthusiasts and it was great to get out and about with the GPS, tramping over the countryside, looking under rocks and in nooks and crannies for the small box left there for fellow Geocachers to sniff out. Sandy was the expert and soon had me looking for the tell-tale signs of tracks leading to the little box of goodies. We signed our names, logged the details on the computer and Sandy gave me a parting gift of my own plastic ducky to come with me on a journey far and wide. Leaving Scotland, I promised to take Ducky on its own adventure. Like me, it would have no home and was going to find itself in unknown places, to be picked up and taken on a mystery ride as far as Australia.

As a visitor meeting up with old friends, there were so many things to talk about and it was easy to navigate the conversation away from my own personal crisis, as I was so happy and light-headed being in the company of such good friends. I did not feel I needed to explain why I was on holiday with no real plans or deadline. I brushed it off with excuses saying Mum was getting old and I wanted to come and visit her. That I would have to come every year now she was in her dotage. Mother would not be amused if she heard how I slathered on her ageing process, and I was really in fear I would bring on her decrepitude with such flippant fibbing. I was becoming a master of covering up the true nature of myself. Onion Girl had years of experience of not fully peeling oneself in public but rather bolster the outer layer with more bravado.

However, at night I lay awake with Lamia in my head forcing me to focus on my future and look at the heart of the matter; the reason why I was escaping my life and sons and how was I ever going back. My onion skin was getting peeled and I did not like the look or the smell of it. Even to myself, I stunk.

I really did not know what to do; all I knew was the path ahead was unknown. I was going with the flow and this was turning out to be a fantastic opportunity. But my heart knew that it would not last, there was a price to pay, and that time was coming. Lamia was whispering in my ear making me feel uncomfortable; my legs prickled and twitched. My restlessness churned up the bedclothes, like a disgruntled sea and I was glad of the early mornings. The dawn streaming in the window at 4am, and the chirping sounds of songbirds calmed me to sleep. It was not going to be easy, making a decision of what was right for me and the boys.

I knew I could not cope with going back to Ozzie. He had spent the last five years working in a thankless job and coming home depleted of all the goodwill, and the cheery smiles I was accustomed to had since vanished from his lips. Instead he poured out the shit of the day as regularly as when I cooked the onions and I felt like this daily dumping was taking its toll on me, as I was subjected to his barrage as soon as he walked in the door.

PEELING REGRET

My newfound freedom gave me plenty of energy and I looked at the world with rose-tinted glasses. Gone were the days of drudgery and dissatisfaction, my life struggling to get to work on time and fighting the desire to drive recklessly into oncoming traffic. I realised how much of an onion I had become as no one really wanted to spend time with me, my workmates would walk away when they saw me in the kitchen, my temper was short, and frustration ate at me from within.

The answer to me was to run away from a life closing in on me as I could no longer see my way out. Suicidal thoughts permeated through my tough outer exterior and sometimes I would find my eyes leaking tears for no apparent reason, raw onion tears.

Ozzie had caught me one day sitting on the sofa, the tears streaming down my cheeks silently, and had asked what was the matter; was I depressed or had something happened. He watched as the tears just wouldn't stop, but there was no sobbing or grief, it was like the overflow just running. The onion tears suppressed for all these years finally bubbling to the surface. I didn't even care; I let them come. Unusual for me as I had spent my entire life trying not to cry. Fighting back the temptation to burst into sobs and screams. For me crying was a weakness, an intolerable act of self-pity, a stupid girly reaction to be avoided at all costs. An act that left me with a splitting headache and unresolved frustration. But in this instance, I was out of control, my onion was beginning to peel its many layers and even though I did not feel sad, my eyes welled up and the tears trickled down my face and there was nothing I could do. Ozzie was struggling to understand and find the right words as I sat there on the couch, while he watched, then when I said I didn't know how long I was going to sit here crying for and that there didn't seem much point in him hanging around, he got up and left me to my emotional breakdown.

The months passed and I had joined art classes, attended new community groups, made new friends, I even tried learning to play guitar, as turning 50 filled me with the strong desire to fulfil myself, take me away from mediocrity and the beige canvas of my everyday life.

I knew it was not Ozzie's job to make me happy and for a while, I tried to find meaning by going out to new meetups and learn meditation.

But at night the meditation techniques did not work, and contempt for the method of relaxation overwhelmed me. How on earth was breathing deeply going to fix me? Letting go of all the stresses of the day as they left my body, like tiny fizzy bubbles bursting from my chest. How was this ever going to help me when all I wanted to do was scream? What was I trying to achieve by letting the wave of relaxation slacken my jaw, soften my cheeks and soothe my aching bones? Did I really believe I could melt away the stress and anxiety that was harboured in my stomach? No, it was impossible, and this sort of self-help claptrap did nothing but fuck me off as it was not that simple. Lamia screeched in my ears at every opportunity and scoffed in my face if I tried to relax. She was being a devil and that meant reckless thinking, riding me around the paddock, leaving me breathless.

I did not really believe I could overcome the impossible by concentrating on my breath. All I could do was let out a huge sigh of exasperation. I lay awake again with no rest - how was I going to get through the day - while Ozzie would sleep for both of us. His snoring grated me to the point I had to leave the bedroom, vacate the marital bed swearing abuse fuelled by a massive dose of sleep envy. It was fucking impossible to stay asleep all night with him and Lamia, who was making me want to commit murder!

The Scottish mornings were fresh, and my week had gone quickly. It was time for me to leave, get on a plane from Inverness to Manchester where I would meet my cousin and stay for a day or two in Sheffield before driving across France to our final destination, Spain.

I sat on the bed and wrote my first letter to Mum in a long time. Over the years, she had sent many letters to me on a weekly basis; it was now my turn to reciprocate. I needed to explain why on the morning I had left for Scotland I had been acting like a teenage daughter cranky and dismissive of her pleas for explanations. I could see that I had left her with that horrible raw and unappealing onion. It is funny how we treat the people most dear in our lives; my mother was such a gentle soul and I have not always been the loving daughter. As a teenager she would stick up for me when I battled my father. She has been my constant ally and it was time to explain what I had been up to. It was time to show her that I cared. But Lamia had other ideas and the letter turned into another lashing.

Dearest Mother

I write to you from my bed in the Highlands. I have seen so many beautiful horizons in this magical land and my hosts have been absolutely gorgeous; I owe Sandy and her husband a huge bottle of whisky for putting up with me and showing me the true heart of Scotland, with its moody and unpredictable mountains, no doubt I could get lost in.

I appreciated your concern as I know you have my best interests at heart, and the fact that I could not explain fully the reason for my sudden arrival has only led to you feeling out of the loop. It was not my intention to hide the true reasons but only that I am struggling to come to terms with them myself.

This is going to be a hard thing to say since I know Ozzie is the apple of your eye and can do no wrong, and I agree with you, he is a fantastic father and has a very deep love for me and his sons and I should not take him for granted.

However, after years of being the dutiful wife, I have taken action and sacked myself as a mother. I have quit the role of homemaker and don't give a shit anymore. And in order for me to find love and self-worth, I need time away from them, as I am not feeling I belong in a long-term relationship anymore. It is as if I am lost at sea, drowning in my own mediocrity, we struggle to talk to each other and there are times when I feel despicable.

Desertion is a very ugly word Mother and one I would not use myself, but you say I should have thought about it, talked to Ozzie before I left instead of just acting out of the blue. Maybe it wasn't such a sudden realisation, as I think I have been planning it all along. I need to escape this humdrum life as it is all too much and for that I am sorry. I know this is hurting the boys and I cannot bear to see the look on their faces as this cuts me to the core.

I will be going away with cousin Lauren for a few weeks to France and Spain and when I return, we will talk this out, as at this stage I do not want to go back to Melbourne.

Sorry, Mum, I know you are really worried and cannot fathom the whys and the wherefores, but can you not see this is for the best, as this is for me. I need to revive myself from a near-death experience. The neglect of my marriage and the erosion of my soul. Please try to understand that it is not just simply my menopause. I hate that word - what have men got to do with it - but I agree with the 'pause' bit as in my head it translates to my need to simply stop and take stock of my life and find my old self again.

Happily renaming it fem-o-pause, as 'the change' has been kicking my arse for a long while now. Perhaps I will morph into a beautiful butterfly, rather than the angry moth that has been terrorising the neighbourhood.

Yours disparagingly,

x Vivi x

PEELING REGRET

Later, on the plane to Manchester, I daydreamed that I was no longer married, that I could do what I liked, meet a handsome man and have uncomplicated sex with him. I laughed to myself to think I was even capable of having an affair, of lighting passion's fire and dancing around it well into the night. Now all things were possible, and Lamia could have her way with me and if I get propositioned, I would have to say, hell yeah!

It was time for me to shed all my layers to become unencumbered by life's expectations.

Feeling free, if this was menopause, then bring it on!

Dear Sister Heart

I have been hiding away in the Highlands, the land that you once knew, and it feels so enticing. I can imagine myself living here and getting a job in Inverness. The quiet solitude has this restorative quality I didn't expect, and I am awestruck by the mountains and lochs. My long-time friend Sandy has taken me under her wing, and I am happy in her company, she has always been a breath of fresh air and reminds me of yourself, bonny and bright.

I know you have been wondering what happened to me and it is only now that I have found the time to write to you, that my thoughts turn to the last time we had a heart to heart.

My dear friend, we have shared so many trials and tribulations and I truly thank you for being my constant companion as you have stuck by me on the long walks and talks about husbands and the misdemeanours they inflict upon their wives, many unknown to them. You have acknowledged my pain and frustration as the world closed in around me.

The last time we really talked, I remember confessing the whole situation, of how I feel I do not count, I am the unpaid worker and that Ozzie is no longer invested in our relationship. He doesn't want to go out with me and spend time reconnecting. This has been a problem and I cannot see my way out of this. I believe that neglect is the number one reason why couples get divorced. And then there is the financial side of things; I cannot afford to leave, split up the home, live on my own. What happens to the boys if we were to divide up our lives? I don't want to think about it, as I know this is beyond me at this point in time.

It has been four weeks now, but time has flown. I no longer have the responsibilities of work and coming home to a house I don't have to clean, and meals I don't want to cook. It has been a revelation. There is even a chance I may just stay a little longer and get a summer job, work in a Devon pub, or get an office job at the cider factory.

Thank you for looking in on Ozzie and the boys, this is my biggest fear that they will all fall to the wayside, and at least you have been kind enough to take some meals around for them.

Be a darling and keep checking in, as this gives me such a comfort when I am so far away and let me know if they are okay.

Your Sister Vivi x

CHAPTER 7

Peeling Freedom

'ONION GIRL LETS LOOSE'

I waited for Lauren at the airport, and she drove up in a brand new Mercedes. I was delighted to see her familiar face and her hugs and kisses were much welcomed. On the way to Sheffield, we talked non-stop and before long we were driving across the Peak District, and an unfamiliar landscape. I was feeling like a southerner in this strange northern land.

Lauren and I were not blood cousins, but our adopted families had very long ties and it was great that we were similar in age and experience. We planned to drive from her house in Sheffield towing a trailer full of furniture to the house in France and then onto Spain. It was going to be such an adventure and she said she would be glad of the company. Lauren ran a small business as a property developer, and this meant we could stay in the unfinished houses that she was project managing throughout our trip. I had never driven on the other side of the road, let alone spoken another language, but Lauren was fluent in French and so I had every confidence in her.

ONION GIRL

After a short weekend in Sheffield with the car packed and the dogs loaded in the car boot, we started our journey. We had our language CDs ready to learn Spanish in 24 hours as we drove to the coast to board the train under the English Channel. The 'Chunnel' would take me further than I had been in many years.

Dear Biddy

This feels strange to me, writing you a real letter when we usually chat on the phone for hours. Well, it is time I shared my little story with you as I know you are busy supporting Mum and helping with her everyday needs. I must confess that I thought I would be more useful in her old age and it would be me getting her shopping in and tidying up the house since you were always the glamorous one.

I really did enjoy our time in the meadow on mid-summer's eve. When we walked to the field behind Mum's cottage with our cider and our snacks, it was great to lie in the long grass hidden from sight and enjoy the slow evening, listening to party revellers in the next village, and the view was magnificent as we scanned the rooftops for our own beautiful cottage that is our mum's home. It was so warm we could have slept out all night and counted the stars in the midnight sky. Heaven was in reach and I loved your company and our singing which must have reached the tractor drivers as they cut the hay late into the night.

Do you remember the badger digging up the muddy lane and excavating all those old Victorian medicine bottles thrown out by some old farmer? We took them home to the cottage and cleaned them up; such wonderful old treasures. It is funny how I think of those days now, how we rode our bikes along the old roads and got lost in the countryside when we were first discovering it for ourselves in the early days as Mum moved into the cottage after

PEELING FREEDOM

Dad died. I got a puncture and had to walk the bike home, and you couldn't manage the hills as they are so steep and at one time I watched as you reeled on the bike backwards. I laughed at your ineptitude, as sisters do.

Thank God for the fireworks. I love it how they lit up the sky and made me realise that you still have some that I left in your attic for a leaving party we never had as the weather was so bad. How I hate goodbyes and in all these years I have never gotten over the fact that I had to leave you all and go to Australia. Find a new home, with my real family left behind. We spoke about many things that night, about how I don't feel I have a home anymore, how I have been a wayward traveller, a tourist, and that I don't belong anywhere. I always imagined a home makes you feel contented, a place to rest and feel at ease. I don't think I have ever had that feeling.

Our childhood home was so uncomfortable, full of the atmosphere of unspoken words, tight-lipped and unpredictable, as we scooted around Dad and his temper. I didn't have my own bedroom but had to share it with you, and Dad was so difficult at the best of times. Is it any wonder we now spend much of our time talking about him, coming to grips with the savage way cancer took him from us before we had a chance to properly reconcile?

You were the apple of his eye, the girl of his dreams, while I was the thorn in his side and the one who would answer him back when he was being strict and unreasonable. Do you ever think we loved him or was it just that we were supposed to feel that we loved him? A conditional love foisted upon us by the fact that he was our father. Did he love us?

Now I am leaving to travel to France and Spain, I must tell you how excited I am to be doing this, but it is not without pain as I know you and Mum would have chatted about my unpredictable attitude to my marriage and the fact that I have left. It is high time I took action as doing nothing has been like gnawing my own arm. You always said I was mad to get married, to tie myself to a man, and I have admired you for not getting hitched and making your life your own. But even with all the financial difficulties, you seem to have found contentment in your life with your darling son.

I am taking time out and will be heading across the Channel by the time you get this letter. We can play our guitars when I get back as I have a few more songs I want to try out.

Let's sing all night next time.

And remember that I am always your loving sister, from when we were young to when we grow old.

Love Vivi x

Calais was a bustle of cars heading in all directions and Lauren navigated through to the customs point and the guard checked our Australian passports. All good to go, we drove the long distance to our new home. France has these wonderful wayside stopping places for cars and lorries with quality facilities to dine and wash in. These are open 24 hours and we find them easy to pull over in and sleep for an hour and eat on snacks before continuing on our long drive to Saintes, which is in the south-west. We are night travellers taking intermittent breaks to walk the dogs and stretch our legs and it amazes me how we can tow a trailer full of furniture and not even notice it. The dogs occasionally whine that they want to get out but otherwise they sleep and are so happy when we finally arrive at the French house in the early light of the morning.

Immediately I see that we are in a quaint village with the delightful stone houses in French narrow streets; we are transported back in time to a more sedate and simple life. I pinch myself as this will be my home for the next week. We quickly get supplies in and are set to open curtains and dust and deep-clean all the surfaces, including the steep staircase, which I scrub with a dirt buster brush. Lauren and I remove the covers from the furniture and unload some of the trailer. It is a ritual we repeat later in the Spanish villa, but it is most satisfying to make the home liveable after months of lying dormant.

The dogs are eager to go for a long walk, so we head off into the sunflower fields, their large daisy heads turn up to the sun, vines grow in rows, flat fields, small lanes, stone chateaus, shuttered windows. This is France, and I love it. My journey has brought me here to this small village and it is beautiful. A peaceful haven for Lauren and her family to retreat and recharge. My boudoir is on the top floor. Scaling the three flights of stairs, I love the old wallpaper and wooden floorboards that creek as I climb up to my room. My bed is large and made of wrought iron and we make it up with pretty flower bedclothes and soft blue pillowcases. I have a round porthole window which overlooks the street below and blue shutters open to the courtyard from the bathroom. My love of France is reignited, and I crave the simplicity, cheese, wine, salad and fresh baguettes.

It is wonderful to breathe in the foreign air as it is now six weeks into my journey and with little Internet access, I am delighted not to be tempted to call home. I relish my journey of self-discovery and reconnection. I am blissfully content and determined not to give in to frustration and ill temperament of menopause as now it is time to let Lamia fully retreat and allow my old self to find a way to the surface.

It is humid and I love the predictable sunshine; it makes the days so slow and easy as we explore the nearby towns. Lauren loves to go bargain hunting and we are soon driving to the local brocante antique markets with the vast array of bric-a-brac and without doubt the best flea market shopping in the world, for those keen on finding treasure from other people's cast-offs. Lauren hunts out an old set of yellow china plates which will go nicely on her French dresser and I love the dusty old barns we find ourselves in.

My joy of cooking is finally returning, as everywhere we go, we are surrounded by the freshest produce and tasty pastries, the best I have ever seen, each supermarket shop an assault on all the senses, and I am eager to try out many of the cheeses, breads and meats on sale.

It is both inspirational and comforting to have Lauren as my guide, as we are starting a new sister relationship which is good for me and I hope that she feels the same. Our histories are already entwined by marriage, a cousin so to speak and it has been years since we really have touched base.

I am still thinking of Scotland as its beauty had seeped into my bones and the wild Highlands a magical experience for me to be bottled, and I appreciated my lovely friend Sandy, taking me under her wing. I am surrounded by such wonderful women; my mother and sister, and my girlfriends back home and now Lauren nurturing me and helping me come to terms with my inner turmoil. It has been years since I felt so loved and it takes me a while to get used to this.

I return to my question of, what is home? I have been so busy making one for the boys, that I forgot to include me in it. The restlessness overtook my senses and the fact that I felt I had forfeited any chance of making a home in Devon when we moved to Melbourne. Since then, I have been homeless, for the past 13 years. So, for now I am happy to be on the road, in the flow; my home is in the fields and the meadows, woodlands and forests, the sea and beaches. I am out in the Universe; my home is in the seasons, summer is coming and going with me and my suitcase. I am in a peaceful state of mind being buffeted in the flow of life by my new experiences and finally I feel like I am blessed to just be me.

Later in the week we went into Saintes and walked by the banks of the river Charente and explored the Roman museum. The town has its own Arc de Triomphe built by Augustus and we walked over the old bridge spanning the river. We sat at tables in the covered market dining on fresh bread and cold meats topped with delicious cheese. I have never seen such a wonderful array of market stalls. I wish I could spend more time there, but we are getting ready to move onto our next part of the trip; Spain. The days go quickly and after a short excursion to the beach at La Rochelle, we have a full day in Bordeaux. I am awestruck by all the buildings, the historic city and the majestic churches. As we are caught in a rainstorm, we head into a café.

Dear Sister Blister

I feel so civilised. Being with Lauren in France has given me a taste for the finer things in life. Good cheese, great wine and fine clothes. Our days are easy; we walk the dogs in the sunflower fields in the morning, take breakfast out on the terrace beside the dovecote and then get ready for the day. Lauren loves to furnish her old house with items bought at the Brocantes, which are antique junk stores, and a paradise for collectors. The prices are ridiculously low, but we end up having to clean the items when we get home, as they are covered in grime. We are the French equivalent of 'American Pickers'. A shame I only brought a small suitcase as there are so many ornate iron beds and giant wardrobes that I can feel a new export business idea coming on.

Driving on the other side of the road has been easy, as Lauren is very adept at navigating throughout France. We spent almost 24 hours getting here to our little village outside Saintes and although I should be tired, I am invigorated. I feel like a local as we stroll around the town and am introduced to a few of Lauren's friends. We ate at a fancy restaurant last night and sat outside on a glorious summer's evening, amongst the historic city with the sophisticated folk, drinking gin and tonics, and although I cannot understand all of the conversation, I can pick up the general gist. We feasted and clinked our wine glasses well into the night, as I was dining with a local celebrity, a cheesemaker who had his name on the menu beside his famous fromage, a delicious goats cheese. Fancy that! Oh, how I love this world and I am not keen to wake up from the dream I have found myself in.

Everywhere I look there are things of beauty, wild flowers grow in the grassy verges as we drive around, and we stopped to have our photos taken with gigantic statues of snails. Very funny, I don't think I can bring myself to eat them yet. We spent a day in Bordeaux, a grand city of majestic buildings and spires, on a huge river. We strolled around the shops and bars until we got absolutely soaked when the dark clouds emptied a month's worth of rain in a minute. We took shelter in a small café and enjoyed a simple lunch of omelette and salad. By now I would have put on several kilos if it wasn't for walking the vineyards with our little furry friends, Charlee and Helia - the most adorable dogs you have ever seen.

I must say I am not thinking too much about my family, although if the conversation turns to them, I do get a pang of guilt, as I feel I have lost connection with them, but it lessens by the day. I guess Ozzie is taking care of the boys, but he doesn't want to talk to me at the moment. His silence over the years of our marriage has led me to make up my own conclusions and the one I have settled on now is that old saying, 'out of sight out of mind'. I hope my sons don't feel the same way. We have been going through a rough patch and I am not sure I can bring myself to come back to him yet. We will have to wait and see.

I do miss our heart to hearts as you have always been such a good listener. Over the years of our friendship we have shared so many stories and been honest about our feelings. So, I owe you this explanation at least.

Taking time away from my family has been the best thing I could have done, since I was feeling so neglected and overwhelmed every day and barely functioning as a parent, let alone as an employee. My menopause has been the massive jolt that I needed, even the restlessness and mood swings aren't affecting me as much, because of this chance to finally breathe. I have forgotten to take the hormone replacement patches for the past few weeks and will now live without them.

Who knew menopause could be so disruptive? It was driving me insane with so many sleepless nights, like having a new baby. Why don't men go through this? You know, the more I live with them, the less I truly understand them. They are like aliens on a female planet that have come to invade our space. Have you ever met a man who is authentic, present and empathetic? I have been searching for a Wiseman, one I can connect with on a deeper level, who can teach me and guide me in things that I am ignorant of. The ones I know seem so shallow. Many men are portrayed like idiots in commercials and the more intelligent ones are quiet and unapproachable, like my dad. But bring out a fart joke or a football game and they become the life of the party. I don't want my boys to end up like this.

I know it is not Ozzie's job to make me happy and I am well aware of the strain I will be putting him under as a single dad. Hello, welcome to my world of all the nights he was away, and I had to put the kids to bed, get them up for school, cook and clean and run the household, alongside my full-time job. It's been tough and giving him a bit of his own medicine doesn't leave me feeling guilty in the least.

But my darling boys are having to fend for themselves too and this worries me. I do hope they are warm at night and getting a decent meal.

I am not even sure I will have a home to come back to as there has been idle talk of changing the locks and perhaps selling up entirely. I could come back to Melbourne and find somebody else living in my house. So, if you should drive past my doorstep, look out for a for sale sign and be a darling and let me know.

Being away is extremely liberating, Sister. If I could, I would spend years travelling around the globe and less of it working from 9 to 5 as a modern-day slave.

ONION GIRL

Life is short and I am only just waking up to this!

Don't you end up living a half-life like me.

Please promise me you won't get married again.

Love Vivi

The night before leaving France to head to Spain, we pack up the car and trailer and sit on the terrace with our wine glasses. I had just cooked spiced couscous while Lauren grilled meat on the BBQ. It was a nice evening and we talked until late.

Earlier I had tried calling home and had been checking emails. There was nothing from Ozzie and the boys and I was now seeing my life in a different way. It didn't matter if I had sleepless nights or menopausal symptoms while I was travelling, as the daily stresses of our day were simply not there. I was going with the flow and being in the moment. Life was good and my cousin had taken me under her wing for which I felt eternally grateful. Another fabulous female - strong, capable and wise. Lauren was an inspiration to me, but it still left the thought in my mind, 'where are all the Wise men?' While women everywhere seem to be coming into their own, was it true that the men were finding it hard to keep up and like Ozzie were shrinking back into their shells like giant snails?

I wanted to find a Wiseman and ask him several questions, like, 'What is love?' 'Do men feel love?' and, 'Is this love the same for them as it is for women, or rather a kind of respect combined with sexual need; a friendship with benefits?'

I could connect on a deeper level with all of my girlfriends, my sisters and my Mother. But with men, it was an empty space, a void. I just didn't have any connection with the men in my life and the question remains, does that come from my father?

PEELING FREEDOM

The last night in France I tossed and turned on the iron bed, as Lamia rose the temperature of the summer night and I sweated into the bedsheets. I lay awake staring at the ceiling and yearned for the touch of a man. A warm embrace, a lover's kiss and a strong sensuous body, towering above me. My arms wrapped around his back feeling breathless.

My Key had not emailed me or sent any messages, and I wondered if I should try to reconnect ? But this was dangerous territory and I knew my snake Lamia wanted more. She was not finished yet but was flexing her scaly body against mine saying 'Do something or die'.

CHAPTER 8

Peeling Inner-Self

'ONION GIRL'S GYPSY SOUL'

Dear Biddy

My daring sister, it has been over a week since I left the UK and I have finally made it to Spain. We left early and once across the border drove over the Pyrenees. The scenery was spectacular as we headed south on the highway to the outskirts of Madrid. Lauren had pre-booked a hotel and after a quick shower, we headed to a small town square where all the locals were eating. Trying out our very bad Spanish garnished from the language CD we played in the car, we ordered our meals and the dogs sat under the table. Not sure if this is doggy etiquette in Spain, as we got a few sideways looks, but that could have been because we are two tourist senoritas making a grand entrance to the land of flamenco, tapas and guitars, with our dogs on leashes. We would have made a peculiar sight.

We ate well and drank our first sangria and before long the Spanish were ignoring us as we scoffed our potato fritters and salad, handing *down titbits to our two companions. Some children came over to say hello to the dogs and it was nice to see them receive the added attention that comes with being so cute.*

Not sure we would get the same reaction without the dogs. We slept so well and left the next morning, packing up our eski. We managed to eat a meagre breakfast before jumping back in the car and driving south towards Granada.

It is hot here - really sweaty - and the scenery gets drier as we head south. Olive trees are everywhere, the patchwork quilts on the rocky hillsides as Spain is the biggest producer of olive oil and if you cut down an olive tree, you have to replace it by order of the Spanish King.

We are now in Alcala la Real, which is a fortified town dominated by a huge castle built by the Moors. Spectacular, the town has fountains in the main square and lovely gardens to walk around. The streets are so old, and I am in love with the architecture of Spanish houses built of stone with wrought iron bars on balconies and large windows, huge wooden doors, tiled hallways that lead you into a central area, with plants and tables. We manage to park just outside the door of Lauren's latest house project; a four-storey home in the old quarter a few hundred metres from the fortress walls. The road is very small and we just about fit in.

I am shown to my room and we have to put my wrought iron bed together, but this time my feet don't touch the ground and I can dangle my legs over the edge of the bed like a princess. We open shuttered windows, take the covers off the furniture which has been stacked in one corner of the lounge room, and we clean. The builders have managed to finish the kitchen, which is great, but other than that, there is a lot of work to be done. Our bathroom is off the kitchen and is down a few steps. The stairs going up to the roof terrace are old, but the views of the town are beautiful. It is so white and bright; I need to wear sunglasses all the time.

We have spent the last few days getting supplies in and cleaning, making it so cosy and moving the builder's supplies down to the ground floor storeroom. The house is now dust-free, and we have begun our daily rounds with the dogs to the olive groves under the gaze of the majestic fortress. We look so out of place here, there is not a tourist in sight, for this is pure Spain. In the evenings we head out late for tapas and Tinto de Verano, a mixture of red wine and sprite. It is refreshing and I love that each glass comes with a small plate of delicious food.

Everyone in the town comes out around 9pm, which is ideal as the heat of the day does take it out of you. Lauren and I like the long mornings, going for walks with the dogs uphill to the fortress walls and there is trackway heading down the hillside. We start a commotion every time we step out the door, as neighbourhood dogs bark and growl as we walk up the old street. But once in amongst the olives, we let the dogs off the lead and Helia just runs free. We don't see her for ages and then she just turns up checking to see where we are, and we give her a drink of water from our backpack as it is far too hot to go anywhere without drinks and our hats.

After our walk, we shower and spend another hour on the rooftop having fruit and muesli for breakfast. This slow pace is just what I need to recharge my batteries. Come the afternoon at around siesta time when it is too hot, we head out and explore, as this time it is quiet in the town and a few of the supermarkets are still open. Lauren needs to find tiles, windows and renovating supplies, so we go to a Spanish hardware store and try to buy tile cutters. Amazingly the amused young man understood what we were saying, but it took a lot of hand gestures and pointing at cutting tools. Another night we spent buying a new mattress for my bed and I was amazed that they still delivered this at 10:30 pm that same night.

The Fortress is lit up at night and we meander around shops exploring the streets below, looking for a new bar to have our nightly tapas followed by an ice-cream. The best flavour is lemon.

ONION GIRL

On Tuesdays the town has a market and I cannot believe how cheap everything is. The farmers bring their homegrown produce and the size and variety are amazing. The market stallholders holler out to the shoppers and I haven't a clue what they are staying, but it is fun, and we have bought olives and cheese, bread, potatoes and new bras. There are no Chinese restaurants here, or McDonald's, and it is so refreshing to find a country so confident with itself that it has no need for food imports. Although we do find an 'arab shop', so it is called, with cheap reading glasses and we buy fans, china mugs, hair ties and undies.

My legs are so brown now and I am looking like a gypsy. I haven't brushed my hair properly in days and my natural curls have gone wild in the sunshine. I don't care; I am not looking in the mirror and wondering what to wear each day. I have little clothing with me, and I seem to be getting along fine with my thongs and a pair of sandals. We have walked miles on cobbled streets. I love that I can get Euros out of the hole in the wall and pay my share of the groceries.

I wish you were with me so we could all be together. Remember when we had a trip to France with Lauren before I went to Australia, and we stayed the weekend in her first French restoration house in Normandy. It was a dilapidated old barn that she made look like a palace in no time. I have a photo of you digging up the veggie patch in your floral skirt and another one of us three outside the Bayeux Cathedral. We were a lot younger then and all our boys were so little. I am not sure I made the right choice by emigrating to Melbourne when I think of what we could have had back then. The boys were little buggers, but a lot of fun, and I loved watching them play together with their water pistols and drenchers, chasing each other up the garden. It was lovely for them all to grow up together and now I am sorry we took it away from them by leaving.

Was it the right thing to do? I don't know, as now I am back here life is so sunny and bright, I feel that I belong again.

I will write again soon when hopefully I will have spoken to Ozzie and the boys and tried to sort a few things out. Like whether I am heading back to Melbourne or not. We shall see as at this point in time I don't have a clue. Each day is a new beginning for me, and I am just going with the flow.

Take care

Vivi x

It was true, my life was so uncomplicated here in Spain, no pressures to do anything and the routine of our life was perfect. The heat of the day meant that most people took long siestas for the afternoon, while we got in the car and explored the region with the Sierra Nevada mountain range near Granada looming in the distance. I cannot believe how many ruined castles are dotted along the hillsides, together with watchtowers and hidden Roman villas. These places of historic interest are unadvertised and although I am sure they don't mind tourists, the Spanish don't seem to want to share their world with the rest of us and keep it under wraps. My favourite town apart from Alcala is Priego de Córdoba as this exquisite place has all the flavours of Spain in architecture, a castle, statues and water fountains which we bathed our feet in, under the foothills of Sierras Subbéticas. You can feel the rhythm of Spain under your feet and I want to take flamenco lessons and buy a new guitar. I love everything about Andalucía, even the heat, and I am looking forward to our night at the Medieval Festival.

I wrote in my diary;

Spain, a hot arid land of sandy rocks made green by the countless olive groves, Andalucía a two-day drive, now I am in the heart of Espana and in the house on the old city road, leading from the fortress to the town. It is comfortable enough. Terrace rooftop stone walls, thick dark corridors, balconettes open onto the street below – four storeys, high, my bedroom at the back. I love it here. Spain is so very different.

We turn heads when walking the dogs; we are so obviously strangers that we stand out. The nightlife is absolutely inspirational, to walk out in the evening to a lively town, everyone coming out to eat, walk and drink, chatting with friends and family. It is exciting and I feel at ease here; even though I have a language barrier, this doesn't seem to be a problem.

Today we saw a group of gypsies in the town square, with their darkened skin, they stood out with a confident gait, I cannot help but stare at them as the head man is such a striking figure. Is it any wonder that girls want to run off with him, as he is a handsome beast? I imagine he plays guitar and sings all night long, while the flamenco troupe stamp their feet and toss their heads back, hands on hips, shouting 'Olay'.

We will get around to the fortress soon enough; you can't miss its presence, high on the top of the hill, massive stones walls fortified and awesome. I can climb it anytime, it's practically next door, but I can wait, we need to clean up the house and shop. The Arab markets look good; still the Moorish influence never went too far.

It's been over seven weeks and Mum's birthday is in a few days. I am drinking in the sites to inspire me. I am nurtured by the culture of each place we go to. Scotland, South Yorkshire, Devon, France and Spain are all great places and all so very different. I am having a smorgasbord of experiences, both culinary and climatically!

I found my love of cooking again, but I miss my boys. I get a pang in my heart when I see young boys in the park playing. Up to boys stuff, as usual, I feel that there is not quite enough heart-felt love when they are not around to fill me with their presence.

I miss physical contact too, perhaps I was spoilt in Australia, did I really have a loving husband? He doesn't email me, and I can't call. All men are quiet, what is up with them, is the Universe slowly turning them off, shutting them down? I have yet to ask a real Wiseman 'what it is to be a man'? I only ever meet wise women as they are everywhere!

PEELING INNER-SELF

My home questions have been fulfilled, it seems I am homeless in the Universe, I belong in myself, self-contained and in control, even temperament. Did I finally learn to chill out and not stress?

Right action is still on the go, to explore truth and justice; it seems so hard to get the balance right. Do one thing for another and there is a price to pay. If I leave my family to explore and re-connect with my true self, did I sacrifice that certain happiness of family life and shrug my responsibilities onto my husband? Ozzie becomes a single father, but my own mother has her daughter back, happy and full of life after all this time of living away in another country.

What would have happened to me if I'd have stayed in Melbourne, not come here at all? Would I find a way to be free from all my stress and anxiety or would these emotions have exploded inside me while driving the car to the vineyard where I would probably have been in a fatal accident?

Will I ever be free of Lamia and her turmoil making me restless? But then sometimes I want to thank her for making me get off my arse and being reckless. Sometimes I want to love her too for being a beautiful demon and making me face my own immortality. Sometimes she makes me smile and sing. *Fucking bitch!*

The day begins with sunlight streaming into my window and onto my face, propped up by the pillows and a lovely cup of tea. The street is getting busy and the horn honks loudly as the baker's van makes his morning rounds and the oldies greet him and buy their daily bread. Time to get ready for our walk; the dogs are watching me put my trainers on.

Now we are off and up the hill we climb, dogs marking our ascent with Helia pulling at the lead, determined, while Charlee sniffs every corner. The olive grove is actually the slopes of the fortress which looms large and is our compass. We meander down the rocky road in dappled shade until we meet the terrace walls and the old road covered in grasses, with seeds that get into your socks and fur. The hills are dotted with almond, figs and apple trees; we have already scrumped apples and the blackberries await a night-time forage. The hillside view to the horizon is olives, a patchwork quilt is laid out in various angles, and you can't cut them down without replacing them. We are in the main olive oil region of Spain and it is fabulous.

The heat drives us back to a shower and breakfast up on the roof terrace. We eat fresh fruit and sit on coloured deck chairs; dogs lie exhausted at our feet. It is already midday!

Market day is Tuesday, and the Spanish stalls are bright, cheap and colourful. I buy a bra for two euros and a fan, some olives and potatoes. All veggies look divine, locally grown; we cannot go wrong. I can't take photos as my camera battery is now dead. But the hubbub and bustle of a local market is a sight to behold. What they are calling out, I have no idea, but we manage to get by anyhow.

Lunch is late; 3pm. I have been making salads every day, a jug of Tinto de Verano and we are up again on the terrace, eating ham, pâté, cheese and fresh bread. Yesterday it was smoked salmon and I am looking through the Mediterranean cookbooks for inspiration and can feel my cooking bug bubbling up again. All of this fabulous fresh food; oranges, olive oil, onions, pineapple, peppers. I am making a colourful salad without actually cooking a thing. Platters of fresh market food, meats and breads, cheese, pickles, olives - a true Mediterranean menu!

I cannot talk about Spain without mentioning tapas. We have been out nearly every night, as after lunch we generally watch a movie or take a siesta, then later go out sightseeing and shopping. But by 9pm it is time for tapas. The bars fill up with Spanish families, teenagers or young adults, oldies too, women meeting up for a chat at the end of the street and many are seated outside their houses or along the small roads, happily chatting to their neighbours.

PEELING INNER-SELF

Lauren has been stocking up on her necessities. Last night it was new bowls, wine glasses, a TV, an electric fan, plastic table cloth, a new stand for the umbrella, batteries and rope. After this, we head to the chicken bar and have tapas, which is our dinner. It is usually served on a slice of bread. So far, we have eaten our way through plates of chicken goujons on bread, ham and quail eggs on bread, chipolata sausage on bread and lemon chicken wings, with no bread, hard-boiled eggs with olives and paprika, baked potato with sour cream, chorizo on bread, pork kebabs, bacon and cheese. It goes on for several courses, not to mention all the Tinto we drink along the way. Sometimes we just get served nuts.

We leave at 11:30pm and the streets are full, tables brimming with Spanish locals drinking, no sign of the economic crash here at all. Stopping for ice-cream, the waffle wafers with cinnamon are yummy and I generally pick a flavour I have never tried before. So far lemon, toffee apple, banana and nuts are great, but the pistachio is very good too. My favourite is lemon.

My hair has never been so unkempt, it is wavy and wild, my skin brown in the sunshine, I don't wear makeup and my clothes are getting boring. Only so much you can pack. But I am so relaxed and happy. You'd think with all the walking up and down the hills in the olive groves or old streets of Alcala, I would be losing weight, but somehow it is not to be. I am the same as ever; what the hell, I don't care, it is great just to be here and enjoying my time away from the rat race. I don't want to go back to the grind. Perhaps I can take a little bit of Spain with me.

Life is too short to get so stressed and involved in mediocre trivial things. I am determined not to get sucked into that mindset again. I am resilient and won't give in to frustration. I will not let myself disappear under the layers of the Onion again. Instead, let the waves wash over me. Tides come and go, and it is inevitable but necessary to cast off all the old thought patterns and restore, renew, and cultivate a lovely peaceful garden of vibrant potential, charged and potent with seed. Love in abundance, wealth and happiness, a simple easy way of life, fulfilled and brimming with new hope and inspiration. Anything is possible as long as I can breathe.

It is time to write again to Mother as it is her birthday, another beautiful milestone in her life.

Dearest Mother

I hope you got my postcard of the Fortress of Alcalá la Real where I am staying with cousin Lauren. We are true sisters of the heart and I am enjoying her company along with her dogs, who seem to be our guardian angels.

Your birthday is in a few days and I am busy finding you small presents from the market stalls where the town folk browse and speak wildly to each other, calling out to passers-by. We bought the biggest tub of olives and bread, but then ended up at the lingerie stall for cheap bras and a new handbag each. There is so much going on here, but the heat can make you wilt in two minutes, so I bought plenty of Spanish fans.

Every morning the bread van beeps his hooter, waking up the whole street as the old Spanish mothers come out to buy their daily loaves and small cakes. What a great tradition and I like it that my day starts with the baker honking his horn loudly, as it gets me out of bed and down to the kitchen to make a cup of tea. Before it gets too hot, we take the dogs to the olive groves and meander along the old road that would have been a wagon route in times gone by, leading from the old gates of the castle and out into the farmlands. It is hot; there are fruit trees, almonds, apples and figs, not to mention olives, really old trees, gnarled and woody but providing much-needed shade as we swig from our water bottles and catch our breath from the steep rocky hills that are the landscape patchwork of fields we explore in.

PEELING INNER-SELF

The fortress is the most interesting fortification, looming on every horizon, a stronghold of massive wooden gates, stone walls built on rock and several towers for lookouts. A grand church has been built inside the battlements, which have been besieged throughout the 800 years of Moorish history. The castle stands proud and is impenetrable, like the other defensive walls I have come across, both literal and ethereal. My own Onion comes to mind, as I have fortified myself in the many layers around me.

We spent a whole day exploring and climbing the many stairs to views of unsurpassed beauty, under the gaze of the fortress. The town huddles in the valley, its small cobbled roads and many terracotta rooftops a muddle of Spanish homes. I love every moment and am overawed with its magnitude; exploring it is easy. The days pass and I can't wait for nightfall as the medieval festival begins in three days. Everyone is dressing up in Arab or Spanish folk costumes and I am looking forward to watching the horse parade.

I know you would love the history here and we have plenty to choose from as Romans left their villas untouched with mosaic floors intact. Lauren took photos of us lying on a concrete chaise lounge, and we imaged the slaves feeding us grapes. We had spent a lazy afternoon being tourists in the nearby town of Priego de Córdoba.

It is great to be free, Mum, and I need this holiday to feed vitality back into my creative soul. I look forward to seeing you again in a few weeks.

Much love and have a great birthday.

Vivi x

ONION GIRL

The medieval festival has begun, with people either dressed up as Moors or Spanish Christian town folk. They walk by our doorway, and many people are sat in seats outside as they watch the town file towards the castle. Lauren and I don't have costumes, but we are lost in the crowds. It is already dark, and the walls are lit up with coloured lights, herald flags fly in the breeze and there are musicians with drums, banging as we enter the old castle.

The market stalls are busy. It is fascinating to see so many people and we lose each other in the crowd. I buy earrings and we eat spit roast pork in rolls and drink wine. There is a stage for musicians, the entertainers are belly dancers, and the strolling drummers are everywhere beating their rhythm as we go. I watch the equestrian show where the Spanish horses are put through their dressage paces; the skilled riders dressed as knights in armour, and then finally the showstopper of the night, the aerial acrobats.

Amazing and fearless, the two aerobatic dancers climb over the tower parapets and sit casually on the ledge, over 200 metres up. I am in fear for their lives and can hardly look at them as the music heralds their descent into the fast expanse of space below the tower. They are harnessed to long lifelines; the wires swing as they begin their aerial dance, my heart jumps and I cannot bear to watch this most daring performance of human puppetry.

I am awestruck as it is the most beautiful acrobatic bravery I have ever seen. I cannot take my eyes off the shadows that the spotlight has cast upon the dancers. They swing out and throw each other and hang upside down and I do not see a safety net. My heart is in my mouth as I am in fear of what will happen if they fall. I am aware that the tower they have climbed is the tallest in the castle complex apart from the church bell tower, and it is treacherous, as we had climbed it earlier in the day and the spiral stairs went up forever.

My Spanish adventure is giving me many pleasures and we go back to the festival a second night just for the experience.

PEELING INNER-SELF

I like the long days and endless nights. Some evenings we just sit up on the terrace rooftop with our jug of Tinto and eat paella cooked on the BBQ. The town is gathered below, and we listen to their music. It is here that I ponder my questions of what to do next, now that I am peeling all my Onion layers, stripping myself of responsibility, identity, homeless, without work or income.

Do I return to my Aussie family as wife and mother and go back to my job in accounts payable, collecting money for a construction firm, where each day I find different ways to get people to pay their bills? Or do I stay longer, explore more countries, free and fearless, travelling on the road, becoming a gypsy, just like the ones I have seen in the market squares?

Can I move back to Devon, in the small village, spend time with my mum and be helpful in her old age, enjoy the company of my sister as we play guitars and lie in the meadows on the sunny days? It is a fantasy, as there comes a time when I must make the decision that affects me and my boys. Face up to the truth that I am not quite done with Melbourne, and there is more of the menopause to come yet. Lamia may be off with the gypsies at the moment and has let me get my rest, but she will be back. Of that I am sure of.

But for now, all I want is to feel at ease and have peace in my life and do the right thing. I want to seek advice from a Wiseman, but I cannot find one, so instead, I speak to Ozzie.

My first contact with the boys for some weeks, I hear Robbie's voice and it is music to my ears. How I love him, my second-born son, and he has just been waiting for me to call. I assure him that I am okay and am looking forward to seeing him again. I have bought him a few t-shirts and I tell him about the festival.

When Ozzie comes to the phone, he is clipped and matter of fact, unwilling to question me on how I have been. He doesn't seem to be interested in what I have been doing or where I am staying. All he says is, 'when are you coming home as you are sending us broke?'!

My body tenses and I feel my stomach tighten, as never before had I noticed how he makes me feel when I talk to him. It is so apparent that I get a physical reaction when he is negative. I want to get off the phone quickly but then I have to ask him how he is, and he goes into a tirade about his job and how overwhelmed he is at the moment, that he is coming in late from work every night. I am worried about the boys, how are they coping. It seems unfair on them and it is all my fault.

I get off the phone and head for the kitchen. I need a stiff drink and we have plenty on hand, as our latest addition to the bar is limoncello, a lovely lemony Italian drink that does the trick and I pour two glasses with plenty of ice. We sit out on the terrace and talk about my options, while Lamia has returned from the gypsies and is snapping her fingers at me.

Later that night I find myself making a booking to fly back to Devon from Málaga in five days' time, as I know that I must get to grips with this situation, but I am not very happy about leaving Spain for it has given me so much already.

So, before I leave, Lauren and I plan a long weekend drive to Seville and Córdoba where I can bask in flamenco and find my guitar soul. The one that has been calling me from my childhood when I used to dance to Carmen by Bizet with a scarf in my hands and stamp about the loungeroom to my favourite Gypsy song.

During the night, I am wide awake and listening to the flamenco being played from a nearby house. It is 3am and no one seems to have gone to bed yet. I love it and hang out of the window as far as I can to see if I can locate where the music it is coming from, as I am tempted to go and join in with the dancing.

Olay, my heart is beating to this beautiful soulful sound that reawakens my need for freedom. I am not ready to go home yet. The tears roll down my face in both happiness and longing and I am in need of passion in my life. Once again, I dream of a strong man holding me in his arms and making me feel alive again. Lamia is awake!

PEELING INNER-SELF

Dear Lamia

Those gypsies have gotten into our blood and made it boil. So much rebellion and eagerness to make our own rules. Chin held high, clicking heals, the flamenco plays loud and fast tonight.

How dare Ozzie trample on my daisies when I have been so careful to make my garden green and beautiful. Every time I am happy and doing the things that I want, he makes me feel guilty. How I am sending us broke- Pah! He never asks if I am well, if I have been having a good time. He never asks a thing about me as he is not interested or is it that he doesn't like it that I am now free!

I will show him - It will be up to me when I return, if I do at all.

My sweet darling Lamia, lead me to my open door as I want to fly away.

Your ever rebelling sister,

Vivi x

ONION GIRL

Before we leave Alcala for Seville, there is a town festival again where all the young senoritas come out in their flamenco costumes and parade up and down the streets. They are of school age and must be from the Spanish dance schools. These beautiful young ladies are so pretty in their dresses and I enjoyed watching them walking past me with such feminine pride.

Earlier in the week, I found a flamenco dress in the second-hand store and tried it on. I looked like a Christmas tree and Lauren laughed herself silly. We were looking for an old phone charger cable as mine had broken. Just as well, as I had no desire to speak to Ozzie again, for a few weeks at least, and Lamia had spat in the dust when she thought about me returning to Melbourne.

The day came when we loaded the cars with the dogs and drove to Seville, a few hours away. It was hot and humid and without the sat-nav we would have got lost. Some days the heat just gets too much and even before we had a chance to look around the old bullring, we were sweating, and our hair was sticking to our heads. I wanted to see the Cathedral and the old Alcázar and explore the city. As I was walking around the walls, I heard the sound of a Spanish guitar being played by a man busking in the Cathedral square. It sounded so good and I watched him skilfully play the strings with ease. I bought myself a CD as a souvenir and to remind me of my last days in Spain.

To keep cool we let ourselves get sprayed by the water mist fountains that are outside of every bar or restaurant. Lauren sat waiting for me in the shade while I went to explore further but the dogs looked unhappy lying on the pavement so I gave in; it was 40 degrees now. We got back in the car and drove to Córdoba instead. Our hotel was in the middle of the old city streets and I loved it the minute I saw all the ancient buildings. The Roman bridge spanning the river and again the old Alcázar with its underground pillared halls. It was a beautiful night and we watched a full moon rise over the river in the sunset and meandered around looking for a place to take the dogs and eat dinner.

PEELING INNER-SELF

The next day we were tourists again and I explored the streets of Cordoba, getting my last fix of Spain before heading out to Granada and then finally back on a plane to the UK. I knew I would miss Lauren and I wanted to thank her, so I left her a letter on her pillow for her to read when I was gone.

Spain had been a fantastic adventure where finally I could be free of all expectations and where Lamia had been placated and pacified as I uncovered my gypsy soul again and enriched my life blood, with vigour and vim.

Dear Lauren

It is not easy for me to leave Spain and I will never forget the many happy days in your company. Our final weekend at Seville, the great city open to explore, hot and humid, what lovely buildings and architecture, the round bullfighters ring, with massive wooden doors leading into the arena, like a Roman amphitheatre. It is old and the most famous bullring of all time as Bizet made it the setting for his opera Carmen.

I especially loved it when we peeked into the many open doors as much as possible, so we got an idea of what lies behind these magnificent entrances. The coloured floor tiles and cool inviting hallways made me wish I owned such a lovely home and I look forward to seeing your own Spanish villa restored to its former glory.

I know that the heat knocked out the dogs who lay unhappily on the pavement, but I was determined to walk around the city centre until it was time to leave. I loved Seville and will come back when it is not so hot, and I am booking us into the best hotel when I come again.

As we drove away, I looked out of the car window, while we played my new CD of flamenco, and I pondered on the city walls and the river. On our drive to Córdoba in airconditioned bliss, I saw three eagles nesting on the pylons and wondered what the meaning was of these giant birds and I am not sure how to interpret this sign.

I don't want to leave Spain, but time moves on and we are now back in Alcala for our last night together and our final tapas followed by a walk around the town eating our favourite ice-creams. When I look back at the pleasure of being in Spain with you, I remember the heat, the tapas, the history and the music. All my senses are awakened and filled with new experiences, ever-flowing through my gypsy veins. I am pacified with the sounds of guitar and a rhythmic beat on a box, with flamenco hands clapping. We are all dancers to an ancient sound, vibrant and alive and I love this tribal passion that is all about the arousal of the soul.

I have learnt to be carefree and now I find it hard to fit into my old self, as some of my clothes are growing tighter by the day. So, I have decided to abandon plans to play it safe and by the book. Reckless and random, passionate and full of zest, I am so happy to be myself again. Vivi has come alive! And I have you to thank for it.

I am now ready to be taken to new places where I can go with the flow, adapt and grow. Foot tap, clap, clap, head throws, shoulders back, shake hips and lick lips. OLAY!

Love Vivi x

PEELING INNER-SELF

Dear Lamia

On my last night here in Alcala I can finally stretch into my new skin. The old one is shed on the floor from a final sloughing.

I thank you for showing me the gypsies and being a wonderful but dangerous inspiration. Tonight I will sleep whether you like it or not and brace myself for the road ahead. The one with the signpost saying, 'Go with the Flow'.

You with your long claws and fractured heart have made me face my demons, my menopausal snake, and my love of self has been resuscitated. I am not living a mediocre life anymore and it is time to want and receive more on the journey ahead.

Passion is on the menu as well as love and kindness, and I thank you for all your efforts to burn me up, buzzing and itching me throughout the restless night. Those days may not be over but I can cope with them a lot better, now I can breathe.

You may not agree with my return to Old England, but it is time…

Come with me if you must.

May we dance the night away in reckless abandon.

Yours beguilingly,

Vivi x

CHAPTER 9
Peeling Deep Skin
'INNER CHILD PROTECTION'

My initial feeling when I got back to Mum's cottage in Devon was one of elation. I was back in my bedroom and I had my favourite Axe Valley to explore. My room was cosy with a view of the farmhouse and the hens made regular clucking sounds from the front yard. In the mornings, I loved to take off and walk along the river, looking for swans and fish. Just being in this magical part of southern England is enough for me, as it truly brings me back to my spirit. My time was my own and I could catch up with Biddy later in the evening when she came home from work. Mum was pretty relaxed as now I was back from my travels we could talk for hours over a cup of tea in the old armchairs. But occasionally the conversation would turn to our dad and I was really not in the mood to be taken down that pathway, as my head was full of adventure, having just returned from Spain.

One evening I had gone over to Biddy's house and we had started to cook dinner and play our guitars, which usually meant the meal was served really late, as playing took over any eating, and after, we just sat and talked about our childhood memories, of Dad and Mum and if we could remember what Christmas presents we got. Amazingly, Biddy could remember so much detail of where we lived, what we wore as children, how Mum did our hair and dressed us in exactly the same outfits she had sewn in funky floral material back in the '60s. Our occasional visits from Granny and how Dad used to sit us on his knee when we were little and play with us. We tried to remember everything about the Christmas tree, the turkey and opening our stockings. We would have a mandarin in the toe of a long sock and Mum would always include a chocolate orange, hair slides, a torch and some funny toys. We loved Christmas, but Dad didn't.

Over the years, Dad became grumpy and sour, and we were ushered out of his way when he came home from work and told to be quiet. There was silence at the meal table and so many restrictions, like no TV - especially after school - no having friends over to play, we had to be very tidy, no slouching, shoulders back, heads up and we asked permission for everything, from taking a bath to eating an apple. Our dad scared us when we were young, and he continued to scare my sister into her teens. But not me, I grew up frustrated with the regime of strict obedience and I rebelled. Needless to say, we clashed badly, and I left home at 17. For years I hated him as there were a number of instances that really shook me out of my childhood, and one particular incident was this.

As a child, I was mostly happy, but by five I had already suffered a disabling illness where I couldn't walk following a bad fever that left me weak, which meant I couldn't start school. Bedridden and alone, I was given disgusting medicine disguised in sherbet that was the penicillin of the day before they invented flavouring. Winter seemed long and I was unable to go outside unless it was to pick up my sister from school where I was pushed in a pram. I felt ashamed when I saw all the other children, as I desperately wanted to be at school too, but I couldn't walk due to rheumatic fever.

So, when I finally got better and could go to school, I remember asking Dad for my dinner money, as children were fed a hot lunch at school. He was in his chair looking unapproachable, but my small, cheerful, brave self asked him anyway. He exploded and pushed me to the floor. I remember my pennies were thrown everywhere and I was made to pick them up, to my surprise. I was hurt as I didn't understand what just happened. I cried all the way to school unsure of what I did wrong and it seemed so unfair. Quite by accident, I knew then that he didn't love me. I was a nuisance, a burden, a child he didn't want, and in order to survive this relationship I had to toughen up.

My first onion layer was put over me, protecting my inner self, as I no longer trusted him and would not approach him again without gauging his mood first.

Later in my life, as a teenager, he bullied and bossed me around until one day we had a massive argument over the bathroom, and he pushed me so far I swore at him. He lost his temper and chucked me out into the street, without shoes or a coat; I even had a wet towel on my head from where I was trying to take a bath. My life wasn't good back then and it has now been years since he died of cancer. A horrible death that I was witness to every day with Mum at his side. We got him through the illness and even though I was not the best of mates with him, I suffered with Mum as he was the love of her life. Poor Mum, she lost her husband, but for me, I just closed him out of my life.

Now we were going over the old times and talking about him again; and it was the one Onion layer I was not prepared to peel off, as it protected me and was still intact. This was difficult to come to grips with as my sister wanted to continue our conversation about love and what it felt like to be loved. I knew my father didn't want children and Mum had told us often enough, which left me feeling unwanted. But not from her, she adored us and made up for it in every way possible, and is so loving and generous, the best mother anyone could ever wish for. But the truth is, I did not miss him and did not want to talk about him.

So, over the years, his influence has not been felt. I had left for Melbourne and my life in the UK was a closed chapter of a book. Until I started contemplating living in the UK again, being with my family. I was not going to be able to avoid talking about my dad forever!

That night, as was the tradition, Biddy dropped me back at the cottage in the dark and waited outside in the car until I made it up to the bedroom, as it was an old house and the stairs creaked, and the shadows loomed in the hallway. But once under the covers, I was safe and sound. But I couldn't sleep; my mind was up to its old tricks again - going over and over things, finding something to latch onto, and that subject was love.

Is it possible to love and be loved? What does that mean? Is it our first primal need, a gift received from our mother? But what does that feel like from our father? I really had no idea. I knew what love looked like from seeing Ozzie and the boys; he was so good with them, ever patient and cheerful. He doted on them.

Mother would say, love just is. Love does. Love forgives. Love edifies. Love pacifies. Love creates all things. Love reveals our true self. Love is unconditional. Love is unending, infinite to all possibilities.

But I knew love could also be destructive, the mirror of love, its ugly twin and so I grew up believing in two kinds of love; one unconditional and the other; crime and punishment love, where you do something wrong and something gets taken away. This also meant that I had to ask what kind of love did I give to my sons and husband? Was it unconditional, or was it crime and punishment love? Had I not just left them because I was feeling unloved and unappreciated? Was this the ugly twin of love that I didn't like to admit to harbouring towards Ozzie and the boys? What sort of mother had I become and what sort of wife?

My night was long and restless, and Lamia was back in the shadows again, blowing in my ear and roughing up the bedclothes. All I wanted was to feel passion, love intensely and be truly alive. Like a flamenco dancer, I didn't want to be mediocre and bland; I did not want to go back to Melbourne. I wanted a lover and I needed to be held in strong arms closed around me. I wanted something that I couldn't have. And where was the Wiseman?

It was a Saturday morning and we had all gone for a drive across country to the craft centre at Broadwindsor in Dorset, where we could treat Mum to lunch and look at the art and craft workshops. I had left a phone message for an old boyfriend earlier in the week to catch up with, as I hadn't seen him in over 25 years. This was done via a friend who happened to have Davey's number. Then came an unexpected message whilst we were browsing the crafts. It was Davey's sister and the text said I had to call Davey next week as he doesn't have credit on his phone. This was exciting for me as I had tried to find Davey for years now, but he was not on social media and I had no idea where he lived. We had lost touch and I was in two minds whether to contact him once I had his number, as we were older now. I wondered what he would look like and what would he make of me.

I made the call on the Monday and by Wednesday I was sitting on a train heading to Southampton, and into the unknown. He was waiting for me at the station. I recognised his figure immediately;

tall and slim and wearing a bright shirt. He always liked to look like he was going to a party. And he had sunglasses on. We greeted and hugged, laughed at each other, as we had both changed with age and the usual wear and tear. But our connection was so natural, and we walked back into Southampton city arm in arm.

We spent the day exploring the old town, the art gallery and the docks. We had a lot to talk about as we both dappled in art and music and had many things in common. He was interested in all things spiritual; his knowledge of Chinese philosophy and martial arts, combined with his artistic talents, made it possible for us to reconnect on so many levels.

We enjoyed a drink or two at the local pub and sat outside and watched the world go by.

This was my Davey, a tall, handsome man, weathered by the world, with an innocent view of life, strong blue eyes and a turned-up smile. We talked about how he had lost his partner to cancer and never had children, his love for his brother and his Mum, who I remember well. He updated me on our friends back in the town where we grew up and went to school - it was a real trip down memory lane for me.

We went back to his flat, which was a small one-bedroom apartment near the train station, and he rolled cigarettes before getting out the old photo album of our days in Amsterdam. We lived there together when I was 19, and it was amazing that he still had the photos of us rolling around Vondelpark, stoned off our heads on weed. Happy days of our youth captured on camera. I was feeling overwhelmed and vulnerable. Davey had great sensitivity and knew something was wrong, so he played music and we danced slowly around the room. Davey's budgie squawked occasionally, and I could feel myself coming apart at the seams. It was too much. All the memories, the photos, the music, the love. It was all still there, and he was holding me and saying how he had never stopped loving me and he knew I would come back one day.

PEELING DEEP SKIN

We broke away when I went to the bathroom to cry. I was not prepared for such emotion. I felt in shock that he could unravel me this way, in such a short time. What I had been missing all these years was a hug, a simple embrace, and Davey's hugs were tight, like a bear. He squeezed and held me firm, with his arms enclosed around me and pulled me to his chest. I could finally let go. It was the best feeling in the world but also very emotional. I was releasing all the tears that I had pushed back for many years, under my onion layers. I felt embarrassed too. What was going on with me?

We talked late into the night and when I told him I was looking for a Wiseman, he said, 'that's me!' And he was right, the Chinese philosophy about life and love were exactly what I needed. I had been over-complicating things, and here was Davey living a very simple life, without much money or food, but was so rich and content. He said wealth came from happiness, painting, and being in nature. My art was important to me and he advised me to get back to it and paint. Stop worrying about things and wake up every day as if it was a new beginning.

I woke up the next morning with Davey at my side and we went to a café for a big breakfast. I returned on the afternoon train back to Devon, full of doubt about what I was going to do next. Should I stay in Devon or move to Southampton to be with Davey, where we could walk the beaches looking for driftwood and make art pieces? Or should I go back to Melbourne and be with the boys or continue my travels and spend more time in Spain, or go to Italy?

The next morning, I spoke with Mother about reconnecting with Davey and how much love I felt for him and that I was considering staying here with her to find work and just be on my own for a bit longer. But Mother had a strong view on the matter, as she did not want me living with her when the boys needed me back in Melbourne. She was fine on her own and could fend for herself, so no good using that as an excuse to get out of motherhood. She told me in no uncertain terms to leave and go back to Melbourne.

I told her Davey was coming to stay for a few days and she didn't seem to mind, but we had better stay over at Biddy's house. I was still feeling very fragile and I started to cry. It was unlike me to be so emotional, but meeting Davey again had set off a flood of tears and I couldn't control them now. Mother took me in her arms and told me, while holding my face in her hands, that I had to go home, no matter what, I was a mother and that was that.

In a way, I felt like she was forcing me to see sense by making it impossible for me to stay.

When Davey got off the train, he was wearing a floral shirt and had that cheeky look on his face. He was so funny, and we spent the whole day in Exeter around the cathedral square drinking outside the old pubs and looking at the passers-by.

Davey is an amazing people-watcher who can talk to anyone. There was a mentally-disabled man who had walked passed us a few times and he was looking lost and Davey shouted out to him 'are you all right mate? It's Davey here'. The poor man was confused, and obviously not sure Davey was addressing him, but Davey kept talking to him like they were old mates, and you could see the physical change in the young man. Davey could reach out to anyone and put them at ease. He is so natural and kind, and I had forgotten how special this quality was in him. Before long, the young man was engaging with us and Davey said he would take him out for a drink someday. The young man left us happy and waving his hands. It was so touching to see.

That night we slept together in the sun house in Biddy's garden, but I did not feel sexually attracted to Davey as we were just friends. All I wanted was to be held in his arms, which he gladly did while we looked out at the stars, but we didn't get much sleep. It was so uncomfortable and the moonlight so bright, without curtains.

Our special treat was a ride on the old tram the next day that left from the village down to the seaside. We had a wonderful day, in the soft morning light. The tram ride took us across the wetlands and alongside the River Axe, with the abundant birdlife and ancient hillforts, and finally down to the estuary and the beach. People were happy and greeted us, we had our photos taken with the tram driver and we walked away arm in arm.

We spent time on the beach taking photos of the colourful beach huts and eating Cornish pasties. We laughed all day long and it felt so beautiful to be reconnected. We sat outside the old pub and with a beer in his hand, Davey asked me if I would consider living with him again. It was lovely to hear this proposition, but I was not prepared for his affection. I could not say yes, as I had the boys to consider at home in Melbourne, and it was in that moment that I knew I would be going back.

It was no use; I could not pretend that the boys did not exist; they were a huge part of my life and I was going back no matter if I liked it or not. I had to face up to the fact that even when I was far away across the world, they were my connection, my home, and compass.

When Davey left on the train that night, tears streamed down both our faces, as we had spent the last few days talking about everything, feeling so at ease with one another. We shared so much, and I promised to stay in touch as he gave me some of his paintings and promised to send me music, art and philosophy to keep me on track. How beautiful Davey is, how understanding and forgiving, he didn't mind when I said I was not sure about living with him and I would have to think about it, as I was not ready.

As the train pulled away, I noticed the sun setting on the track and thought it was time to make my decision; it was time to call Ozzie and the boys and say I was coming home.

Then I suddenly remembered I missed my son's birthday – it was not even a day later but a whole week!

Dear Sister Blister

It has been a few weeks now since returning from Spain and so much has happened since then. My life has taken a dramatic turn as I met up with an old boyfriend recently and we went on a whirlwind romance together, reconnecting and filling in all the gaps for the past 25 years.

He is amazing, a lovely gentleman, so wise and happy, an artist and a music lover, he collects songs from all over the world and I have listened to much of his collection already. But while we were dancing to Neil Young, 'Harvest Moon', I seem to have had a meltdown and poured tears on his shirt. I am not sure where they came from, but his hugs and kisses made me melt in his arms. I couldn't believe he still felt the same after all these years and I was overcome with emotion.

We spent the day reminiscing about our life together in Amsterdam where we lived for three years and neither of us could remember exactly why we split up. But sadly, I do not feel a sexual connection to him or to anyone and so we left that side of the relationship in the past.

Darling, I am not sure what I want to do, as it is so tempting to just stay here and live with him in Southampton, collect driftwood, and make art pieces, paint the landscape and explore the New Forest, which I love.

Biddy has warned me to stop being such a teenager as this is about our past love and not the future, and perhaps she is right. I cannot believe that we met after all these years as I had been trying to find him but to no avail. Now he is here, and I am not able to contain myself.

I know my heart aches for his friendship, but I must make a decision about the boys. We did not talk about Ozzie at all; he wasn't even

PEELING DEEP SKIN

brought up in the conversation as I steered it away from my personal life, just to be on the safe side.

Hopefully I can get you to talk some sense into me as I am out of my head again and back in the menopausal madness.

Love Vivi x

CHAPTER 10

Peeling Reality

'ONION GIRL GOES HOME'

When the dust had settled and I was more in control of my emotions again, I could see the path ahead and it was foggy. I had spoken to Ozzie and the boys early evening Melbourne time, my Monday morning, which gave me a chance to sleep off the crazy weekend with Davey and collect my thoughts.

When Ozzie picked up the receiver, I got the same sinking feeling in my belly, as he was sounding so down. I had been away from him for over three months now and the gap between us seemed to have widened to a void. How I was ever going to fit back into my old life again, I did not know.

On the one hand, I wanted to be a mother and finish what we had started, return to Melbourne and get the boys through school fully prepared to go out into the big wide world. But on the other hand, I wanted my freedom to do what I wanted, to explore my life in the UK, the one I had left behind for Ozzie and be with my mum and sister, the long-held dream of us all living close by. And then there was this desire to be held again, feel special to someone else, be desired and loved and free to choose a lover. I wanted that gypsy passion I felt in Spain to flow through me and it needed expression.

Did this mean I had to divorce Ozzie, sell the house, divide our finances, split up the home? I was now dealing with really serious life questions and I wanted independence.

My book club girlfriends had written to me via email and were looking forward to seeing me again, my workplace had got a temp in and Ozzie was asking me when I was coming back so he could let my boss know. So, I still technically had a job and could earn an income, pay the mortgage and carry on as usual.

But my head and heart were torn in two. I did not want to return to Melbourne; it was a threshold I was not prepared to cross again, the flight, the long hours in limbo, my return to the house I had left. It all felt wrong. I was not the same person I was when I left, I had gained a new perspective of myself and my life was returned to me full of opportunities.

I spoke to mother again and told her how I was feeling, and she was sympathetic but kept saying 'the boys need you' and 'you cannot live here'. I was being kicked out all over again, no home to stay in, no place for me. My happiness depended on what to do next and so I gritted my teeth and decided I had to face the music. It was time to get on that plane and fly back to Australia.

This now bought new emotions to boiling point, as many times I had come to Devon and stayed with Mum, only to have to say goodbye to her, leave my sister to be a single mother again and perhaps never see my mum again. She was getting old and counting the birthdays, and in order to get through this ordeal, I had to steel myself, toughen up my onion skin again and pretend it was not killing me. I truly hate doing this, every time I leave, I see my mum's face before me and look at her closely so I can remember everything about her, and then walk away as if I am going down to the shops and will be back in a few hours, not leaving on a plane to fly halfway around the world. It is not easy for me, it is the toughest goodbye there is and I hate it.

Biddy makes it easy for me as she is so supportive. Later that night we take an evening walk through the fields to the river and talk about these being my last days here. I am reluctant to leave her, and I am seriously thinking of cancelling my plane ticket. I had organised my flight earlier in the morning, as I had originally bought a return flight with the date of September. I wanted to extend it indefinitely, but now it looked like I was going back to Melbourne on the exact date I had inadvertently selected.

My whole body was feeling down; my energy was drained, I had been living on a high for so long, with not a care in the world. I had cast off all my responsibilities, shed my identity, and shrugged off motherhood these past three months while peeling my onion layers and now I had to put them all back on again. It felt like putting on clothes that didn't fit. What was going to happen to me when I got back to Melbourne? Could I face Ozzie and go back to living a married life again? The easy part was getting back to being a mother again, as I loved the boys and wanted to be there for them. But somehow the rest of my life was the foggy road I had been driving on in the very beginning of my journey and the meltdown I had on the way to the vineyard. I was going back to square one where nothing had changed.

I had to be strong if I was going to do this, I had to make myself go back to Melbourne and if there was anything wrong with the flight, the train ride, delays, or any obstruction in my journey at all, I was turning around and coming straight back to Devon.

ONION GIRL

Dear Lamia

Are you placated now? Like hell you are. I hear you slamming doors and banging on the ceiling, screeching in my ears, chiding me, your voice a mocking high-pitched whine saying, 'Why the fuck are you going back to Melbourne?'

The answer is simple. I am a mother first. It is who I am. You cannot make me turn my back on this. So you can take that smirk off your face and help me be what I want to be. True to myself, with love and compassion.

I am not going back as the old me, but the new one.

The one you helped me realise.

Me, as Vivi.

The day came for my last goodbyes, with mother leaning over the back door, which is a stable door so she can stand with her arms leaning over the bottom section. She smiles and we take photos with our heads together; my beautiful mother and me. Biddy drives me away and I look out the car window as the countryside recedes into the background, as every inch I am taken away from my Devon life. I am in acute pain and sorrow. I can't believe I am doing this trip in reverse and remember how happy I was to arrive in this sunny heaven. Now the train pulls away at the station, I turn my head and let the tears roll down; waving goodbye is the hardest thing to do. I have never felt so desolate in all my life. I don't care that passengers are watching me as I choke back sobs. My journey back home better be easier, or I am not going through with it.

At the airport, I called Davey and we chatted until my battery ran out. He was supportive and funny, saying he would write to me and send photos. Our happy days together were a bonus I was not expecting, to feel such love and warmth from him. He was the Wiseman I had been looking for, but not my lover. This passion fire was smouldering under the surface with Lamia whispering in my ear. She wanted me to get a new lover, have fun and live carefreely. I had to stop these feelings from taking over me.

The journey home was so easy, no delays, no hold-ups, easy travellers, time went by and it turned out to be the best flight I had ever had. I couldn't believe it and there at the airport waiting for me at arrivals were my beautiful sons; my young men, my darling boys, my life. How much I had missed them. We hugged and kissed, and we fought back the tears and I noticed how tall they both looked, so handsome. My heart leapt and I knew it was for the best. Mother had been right all along; I had to come back to Melbourne for the boys, as they were my life.

Looking at Ozzie though was a whole different story; he was older, and his beard had grey hair covering his face and he looked scruffy. I couldn't believe it was the same man. What had happened to him? We spoke and chatted on the way home to Eltham and it was so nice to finally get back into my house. The kitchen was clean, the dishes put away, fresh sheets on my bed, the house was so tidy. There was food in the pantry. He had taken a day off as it was still early morning. I eventually got back to bed and slept for the rest of the day, but I awoke to cooking smells and their usual voices. The feeling of being in my own bed came over me and I was happy to be home.

But not everything was rosy; I still had to deal with Ozzie and our relationship. I had pushed him to the brink and now needed to get back on stable ground again. We had to talk about how we got to this place in our lives and was there a way we could continue.

Our January wedding anniversary was approaching and although it was a few months off now, I had promised everyone a party. 25 years of marriage and I was not sure I was going to make it to my own event!

ONION GIRL

Dear Mother

It was so good to receive your letters and I love that you are back to writing to me every week. This must have been hard for you when I was living in the cottage as I know you are keen to put pen to paper. Maybe next time you can pass me notes from across the room.

My life has returned to normal and I have been back to work now, where all the girls missed me, and I was soon back in the swing of things with Ozzie and the boys. You were right about coming back to Melbourne, as I knew in my heart, I had unfinished business here and it was only a short break that I needed to restore my vitality and breathe new life into my creative soul.

I have taken up oil painting lessons again and will start to play guitar more seriously as I have a number of songs I want to write and play. The time with you has been just what I needed, and the boys have grown so much in my absence. Both can now cook pasta and wash their own clothes. Ozzie has done a great job looking after them and showing them how to manage on their own and has even started a new veggie garden.

As for my menopause, well, it is still keeping me awake at night, and I know I must try to get to bed early and eat properly. I do miss walking around the country lanes and will be back before you know it, as I want to collect grass and make more baskets for you.

Ozzie and I are planning our 25th Anniversary soon. Lauren and hubby are coming over to celebrate with us. I thought I must be the only person still married after all these years, but apparently not.

He eventually shaved his beard off after his mother rang me to say she didn't like it and was glad I was home. But it took my darling girlfriend to finally persuade him to get rid of the rug on his face when she said he looked like Saddam Hussein. I think Ozzie was waging his own personal war at the time of my absence and we have

PEELING REALITY

a number of things to still get through. But the fact that he looked after my boys while I was away means the world to me.

Thank you so much for being so supportive of me and for giving me the kick up the arse I needed. Without this, I don't think I would have had the strength to come home.

Love and kisses

Vivi x

CHAPTER 11

Chopping Onions
'A CELEBRATION'

I had a huge resistance to coming home to Melbourne; I hated getting on that plane and looked for every excuse not to. If there were delays or if I saw any sign of difficulty with my journey ahead, I was turning around and heading back to Devon. Not that I didn't want to see my boys again, but the fact that I had changed in a huge way was concerning me. Fear of turning back into my old self, of being unhappy again played on my mind constantly, and the question of what was I going to find when I got home. Would the boys accept me as I am? Would I find love for Ozzie again? And would I feel content with my life, or would anxiety smother me as I went back to work, regained responsibility and shouldered the hormonal challenges ahead? Let's not forget, I was still hugely menopausal, and Lamia was stalking me at every turn; she wanted to turn me into a resistance fighter, a creator, an independent being.

I had tried to find many excuses of why I should stay in England, look after my mother in her old age, get a new job and fulfil my desire to continue with my travels. But there was no getting away from the fact that I was a mother here in Melbourne with two beautiful boys and it was my task of being a parent, of raising them, that sent me back to the family home. Mother was right, I was their mother and they needed me. And I needed them.

So, when Ozzie collected me at the airport, I was apprehensive, to say the least. Tired after my long unencumbered journey and seeing him again, with his beard and grey hair, older looking and a bit dishevelled. I knew we had our work cut out for us if we were going to be on the same page again. He did look like he was running on half empty and I could see the relief on his face when I said I would return to work in a few days.

Ozzie had kept the house fairly clean and organised the boys in every way. I admire this in him hugely, as there is nothing he wouldn't do for them. But I had changed and did not feel like the same woman anymore. My time away had erased my thorny edges and put me back into the flow of my life. I was heading downstream and wanted to stay facing in the right direction. But this made me wary of getting back into old habits and I knew Ozzie still had these in abundance from being unhappy with his job. His habit of off-loading all his work issues on me and his negative view of us never getting ahead and making progress in our wealth and well-being.

I knew I had to remain calm and focus on myself if I was going to survive the transition into my new life as this was going to be a real challenge. I had to try to come to terms with my loss of freedom and avoid feeling overwhelmed with emotion when everyday tasks got on top of me. So, I set myself goals to find new things to do, I would start looking for opportunities and friendships and of course, catch up with my lovely girlfriends and book club mums.

Work had improved. Gone were the days of trying so hard to make it to the end of the week as there were so many tasks to do each day, with my job of collecting money for large constructions projects.

CHOPPING ONIONS

But while I was away, new building jobs had come in and were making money, and payments were being paid every day. It was certainly a huge change from before I left when no one was paying and we struggled to move the cash around the business to pay all the subcontractors, while I got on the phone to hassle and cajole people into paying for the work. This was highly stressful, and I hadn't realised just how much this affected me, but now it was so much easier, and my accounts team girlfriends were so happy to see me. I loved being back with them and seeing their beautiful faces light up as I walked in the door. We immediately got back into having morning tea and after-work drinks; any excuse to be social and fun. My next job was to catch up with everyone and tell them of my travels. My soul sisters wanted to hear all about Spain and the UK, and it was fun seeing them all and hearing all their news.

My boys were also my priority, socialising with them again and being involved with their activities with all the usual fun things parents do with their kids. I tried to get into the swing of things and to feel blessed that I had just spent over three months away with all the freedom in the world. The boys were settled and happy to have me back and looked forward to my cooking again, as they were tired of Ozzie's ad hoc way of putting ingredients together; a bit of trial and error in the cooking department. They even enthusiastically offered to come shopping with me as they loved the thought of getting their favourite food. I felt so appreciated in that moment.

But sadly, not all of life was working for me here back in Melbourne. I had to try hard to find the good things in life and feel the abundance of opportunities and not get stressed again. I took up meditation and art therapy classes and played guitar and continued with my still life oil painting lessons each week. I filled my life with activities and creativity and tried to ignore the menopause pain of restless legs, sleepless nights, irritable mood swings and hot flushes at work. I still felt Lamia stalking me at night, but it wasn't as strong, she was now slightly tamed and less threatening.

On the horizon was our 25th wedding anniversary, a day to celebrate my long marriage to Ozzie and say to the world we have made it. But in my heart, I was saying I have done my time, spent most of my life with one guy, and now I want my freedom to do what I want when I want, without all the hassles of divorce. So, one day down at the beach, I made up my mind to write a declaration of independence. A final Onion Girl letter that I would send to Ozzie and ask him to recognise that I was free to do as I pleased, and I would never ask permission to do anything. Not that I ever had asked for his permission before, but there was always an undercurrent in my mind from my days of having a strict father.

The declaration of independence meant a lot to me as I really felt women around the world have so many expectations and have been dictated to for so long; it was time to take control and what I wanted from Ozzie was to recognise this as a Wiseman. Oz has always accepted what I did anyway, although he had blocked my attempt to move to Devon when the boys were little, which ended up in us coming to Australia. I just wanted him to acknowledge my transition from girlfriend to wife, to mother of his children and back again to Vivi, just me. Lamia was pleased I had come to this conclusion and encouraged me to be bold and express myself.

Also, I wanted him to appreciate all that I have done in our relationship, from working full-time to raising our boys, to sacrificing my life and family to come to Melbourne, and to agree not to introduce me as his wife anymore, as this was an old-fashioned title that was redundant in my eyes and I wanted to sack myself as a wife entirely. But in doing this, I also did not want to give up all that we had worked for both financially and personally, get a divorce, split up the home, put the boys through this upheaval. When I told Ozzie of my intentions he laughed and said, 'So now what do I call you when I need to introduce you'? I replied, 'Just say this is Vivienne my house associate.'

I also had a party to organise; I loved celebrations. I planned the catering and the theme was silver, so everyone had to wear something or bring something in that colour scheme. It was so good to have a house party, with my closest friends and in-laws coming over to cut the cake, dance, sing and have fun. I have always had parties at my house; in fact, my 50th Birthday party was the best party ever and everyone came dressed in costumes with the theme, the Best of British. How fantastic this was, and I was excited to see everyone again, including Lauren, who was coming over with her husband, as it was her 25th wedding anniversary too.

The night arrived and we were all gathered in my kitchen, the party lights flickering and the music setting the scene. All my book club girlfriends had turned up and I was feeling so loved and appreciated to have them here, to celebrate this huge milestone with me, as not long before I didn't even believe I would be coming home again. The boys were making themselves scarce as usual as they hate too many adults in their house, but I was feeling excited and blessed to have all these wonderful people around me. Some even bought me gifts. I was not looking forward to the upcoming speeches as I knew I would announce that I had completed my life sentence of 25 years of marriage and was now sacking myself as wife, and I knew that everyone would think I was joking. But in my heart, I saw that my marriage had reached its conclusion and that I had completed all the tasks in my inbox. I was done with marriage and it was a marvel I had made it this far. Lamia was still lurking in the shadows and she would bristle under my skin every now and again.

Ozzie was back to his happy-go-lucky self - the kindest man on the planet - singing my praises and saying how much he loved me. I should be feeling love and appreciation for him in return, but I was still not quite ready. But in that moment, I knew we could get through this transition period and find our way back to being best mates again.

Being married for 25 years, it becomes hard to see all the good things that life has given you. It takes a real effort to continue to appreciate all that you have achieved together. I still can't believe I got through this period of my life, but I must say the best part was that feeling of complete freedom of finally becoming Onion Girl.

So, here is my Declaration of Independence.

ONION GIRL

Dear Darling Ozzie

The sound of the surf, crows and seagulls and a shady spot to write and to explore a small subject. The gulls have taken to sitting around the resident seal who is lying on the beach at Dromana.

I will begin this letter as this pen has potential and what letter should not be so easy to write, but one that begins with dear darling? I will try to keep my handwriting easy to read, as even I have trouble translating my messy scrawl.

The new year has begun and many hours after the fireworks and drunken celebrations, does the enormity of the year itself stand before me. To find a new job, a new direction and a new me. Transformed into the unabridged edition of myself. Christmas Day seems so last year already, and I smile remembering the look of bewilderment on your face as I announced my intention of no longer wanting to be referred to as 'wife or partner' and the discussion that ensued along the lines of 'now what would you prefer to be called?'

'Is it okay to be partner'? No, as it sounds like I am gay. 'Or how about better half'? No, as that is a cliché. 'What about mother of my children'? Hmm no, that is obvious, but also a little sexist.

We put it to our friends who also had trouble finding the word, or a title for She who is married but does not want to be called 'her indoors', 'the misses', or 'wife', or anything remotely related to my status. It isn't exactly a rebellion against a patriarchal society, as our friend put it, but more against our society on the whole for issuing everyone with labels just to make themselves feel comfortable and give them a better viewpoint of the judging they are about to do on my behalf.

Given that I am married to you and not in need of a divorce, as this would split up the family and our home, sharing what little wealth we have and dividing the family unit, the boys, our in-laws, out-laws and me. I would rather have the status quo and I am not entirely happy to being separated as this would mean I have to move out, pack my things and live independently, whether I can afford it or not. A dilemma many women find themselves in throughout this fair land and sending even more of them into poverty.

So, we agree we are to call each other 'house associate' which as I remember got quite a giggle at the time and was meant to be said tongue in cheek. But really all I want is a declaration of independence. A letter or statement endorsed by us both, recognising that I am entirely independent and that I have discarded my shackles, unencumbered by the status rules, I am a whole person, and I can go where I like when I like with whom I like.

Stating the obvious, as I already do this with ease and quite rightly so. As you have pointed out, you have never stopped me in anything. However, I have been persuaded on many occasions to see your point of view, when now I am empowering myself to disregard this entirely. This makes me laugh as I know it is open to interpretation. And the question remains, what has driven me to want this so-called declaration of independence and what does it mean? This is what Onion Girl says....

I have been married to you for 25 years on 11th January, our boys are almost all grown up and I am no longer required to be there 24/7 and have no desire to be the domestic help around the home, cooking, cleaning, shopping and supplying the means of our daily bread. I no longer want to be relied upon to fulfil my duties as wife, and I don't want to make your side of the bed or wash your dishes. You can do that for yourself. It's not just about my domestic goddess home-maker role, but more of me feeling free to explore the world and the Universe externally from pillar to post and also internally – head, heart and soul. I want to be recognised as Vivienne, independent woman. A role model to myself and other women, both young and old and I want to cast off the shackles of marriage without losing everything that I have worked hard for, and also, I do not want this to affect my boys who are the life and soul of my heart.

I sit here unable to express fully my intentions, only in challenging the normal societal view of the current status - be it married, single, separated, or divorced. I want to add a line for the independents which means I can be self-sufficient but also married. I don't have to declare either way!

This sounds like a new political party. But as I watch people walk to the beach with their umbrellas and deck chairs, kids paraphernalia, I am in need of sand myself and a new beach to sit on. I wonder how you put up with my crap, but it is worth mentioning that I have had to listen to your crap for years and I am sick and tired of it. I lay in bed this morning in a kind of meditation purposely detaching myself from the various labels life has put on me, like a menopausal female, over 50 and fucked.

So, have I just declared a new marital status? No, I don't want any status at all as I hate putting Mrs or Ms in front of my name. I am just declaring my right to independence, and no longer have a need for status. It says to the world, just call me by my name.

I declare to my 'house associate' that it is entirely my decision to be independent. I relinquish my role as wife, spouse and partner. We no longer have the right to refer to one another as my husband or my wife, as we are independent, not dependant.

Radical thinking, I hear you say. This declaration does not in any way take away my rights as next of kin, nor does it relinquish in any way shape or form my responsibilities to my children. I am still fully entitled under the law of this land to my fair share of our property and assets held in both our names.

CHOPPING ONIONS

I'm feeling a little disgruntled and I know that the storm clouds will pass. You can put this down to my menopausal madness all you like, but it remains the same.

I am no longer your wife.

But instead, your dear House Associate

Onion Girl x

CHAPTER 12

Onion Girl Sprouts
'NEW SHOOTS'

My Dearest Friends

Having now stripped Onion Girl down to my old self again and declared myself independent, I am ready to create and go with the flow and I am mindful of the contrasts; when anxiety forces me against the tide and my head swoops on negative thought, I try to bring things back into perspective and appreciate all that I have. Resuming to normal life during the last five years, following on from my return from England, I have travelled again on a journey of self-awareness and this turned out to be the homecoming I have been looking for.

Right action is always a challenge; you have to do what you need to do at the time, what feels right for you and sometimes that means making decisions that are only good for you and your survival. This was true for me when I was so very tired and exhausted with Lamia and my menopause.

I have to acknowledge that being kind to myself is the biggest lesson I have learnt along the way. Not to feel so guilty over everything I have ever done, when my life-changing decisions have affected the people I love most, as I have carried this burden for too long.

If I could have planned my menopausal adventure differently, perhaps I would have saved more money and continued to travel in complete freedom of being in the flow and not knowing where I was going from day to day. But timing was not on my side and I had a family that was a priority, and I am glad I made the decision to return to them all.

So, my question to you is, what if your menopause could be different, something to plan for and make use of? What if you could take time away from your family and relish just what living for yourself every day would be? Make the most of every moment and look forward to a bright new future. Come back refreshed and full of vigour. What if you could embrace the changes and just let your body do what it is supposed to do without any intervention?

I wish all women could look forward to their menopausal journey and not have it foisted upon them suddenly with the inconvenience and shame it brings. Perhaps we could all look at this metamorphosis with a new positive attitude and celebrate what a great time of life this is for women who have come of age with love and compassion instead of scorn. We really do need more positive role models on this pathway as there is nothing worse than feeling like a raw onion.

I am so appreciative of Lamia who gave me the shake-up I needed, and although she was tough in her love for me, she showed me I needed to give myself a holiday and find my inner strength again. To breathe new life into my worn-out body and make changes to myself, embrace the new cycle with joy, and take a well-deserved break. I needed to rest and recuperate my creative energy. A pause in my life which turned into a newfound independence.

So, when it's your turn to be **Onion Girl**, say to yourself **'I am ready, bring it on'**.

Final Words

Within six months of returning to my life in Melbourne, a bigger disaster was on the horizon, one that affected my mother, and that was the fire at Stanley Cottage. Coming to terms with the devastation and to see my own mother lost, without a home, the distress of not having anywhere to go, without her belongings and having to adjust to living out of a suitcase with the burden of homelessness and the great sadness that left her breathless from her smoke-damaged lungs.

I had to come to the realisation that life is short and sweet and bad things can happen in an instant. I am truly grateful that she escaped and was not harmed in the fire, having fought the flames bravely, cold wet and tired. It was now time for me to step up and be the strong daughter she deserved and help her put her house back together so she could move back into her home and live out her final days in comfort. Once more, I returned to Devon.

SOMETIMES (Song by Onion Girl)

Sometimes I feel alone, I've lost my home, I don't know where to roam
Sometimes where do I belong?

Sometimes I burned my fire, I've lost desire, the smoke it chokes in me
Sometimes let it burn, burn away my fears.

Sometimes the rain pours down, I want to drown, wash away my tears
Sometimes the endless sky, I want to fly. I'm soaring way up high
Feeling free, blue skies beckon me.

Sometimes I plant a seed, create a need, and inspirations flow
Sometimes I paint the night, with colours bright, the stars they glow
And when its time, I know to let it go. Let it go.

Sometimes I hear a sound, underground, can't seem to keep it down
Sometimes my tightened skin, an itch within, I scratch myself alive
And all the bees, they hum and drum, my seams have come undone.

My Menopausal Symptoms

Sleeplessness
Night sweats
Restless legs
Joint pain
Fatigue
Hot flushes
Panic disorder, anxiety and breathlessness
Depression
Mood swings, temper tantrums, road rage, tearful episodes
Dry skin and pimples
Itchy arms, ribs cage and stomach
Overactive bladder
Headaches and migraines
Memory lapse, confusion, disorientation
Fluctuating menstrual cycle
Libido changes, increase/decrease
Bloating, digestion problems
Hair thinning and greying
Weight gain
Dizziness

ONION GIRL

Urinary tract infections
Brittle nails
Loss of self-esteem

To name but a few….

But a new sense of something great was going to come out at the end!
So, Bring it on!

If you are experiencing any of these symptoms I advise you to seek medical advice and go in search of what is the right action for you.

Acknowledgements

To my mother, your creative, industrious soul has been my inspiration. You are my guide in times of fear and loneliness. I rely on you constantly and know you will always be my lighthouse when I am lost at sea.

And to my wonderful 'house associate' Ozzie, who has been my best friend, a Wiseman and constant companion, a shining example to his sons of what it is to be a man and support his family, with love and kindness and for respecting me for who I am. I feel truly blessed.

Testimonials

Onion Girl is an inspirational book by Vivi, where she allows the reader to feel and associate with her through her anxiety, frustration, pain, guilt and fears as she heads into menopause.

Menopause is an unchartered area for many. No-one's experience is the same. To be able to feel free without guilt, anxiety and other negative feelings towards either yourself or your family would be a wonderful journey, but as Vivi has shown us, this is not possible without judgement.

Throughout the book, Vivi has opened up her heart and life to us all, which in itself is difficult, and from her relatable experiences and adventures, we can all learn to help not just ourselves but others who are in the same predicament; shed our own onion layers as Vivi did and find the real self within.

Carol Nevill – Art Therapy Counsellor

Vivienne Mason's book Onion Girl is a fascinating *'step into someone's head'* about going through the trials and tribulations of both a long term marriage and the menopause, both of which I have some personal experience! Vivienne has captured a lot of the self-searching and confusion of this sort of life experience which I can profoundly relate to. I loved her amazing frankness, which leads the reader to honestly believe they are a close friend. Viv seems to have come out of her experiences of that time with her sensibility and soul intact, which I can only congratulate her for, as it is, I think, as a direct result of her own hard work. I hope on the way she has had some great adventures (I felt like sometimes I was there with her!) and managed to enjoy a seriously trying stage of life for most women! Well done girl!

Allison Robb - Entreprenuer

All stages of our lives can be challenging.

Ms Mason delivers a heartfelt message to all women transitioning through a particularly daunting one. She shows us how we can dry our tears and avoid the pickling process.

Anne-Marie Wilkinson - Registered Nurse

TESTIMONIALS

Lamia is alive and well. I should know because I've also been touched by Lamia. In fact, most women aged 45 years and over have too - she gets around does Lamia!

Vivi has captured the essence of this mythical creature in Onion Girl. Peeling back the layers of her life, frayed by the presence of her nemesis, Lamia, Vivi has documented this raw account of a very challenging time. It's all there under the layers. Her loves, her family, loved ones lost, and the hurt and resentment that often accompanies them.

I thoroughly enjoyed Onion Girl, especially the way Vivi has learnt to live with Lamia while retaining her self-worth and confidence. She has shone through, as I knew she would.

Toni Clark – Manager, Communications and Stakeholder Relations

About the Author

Born in Farnborough, Hampshire in 1962, Vivienne moved to Australia in 2002. She is married and has two sons. She is a self-taught artist and over the years has been involved with many makers and creators around Melbourne; volunteering at Montsalvat and Eltham Fine Art Studio and Gallery, where she was taught still life painting by well-known artist, Jenny Mitchell.

She is passionate about creativity and art therapy practices and has hosted workshops to explore the inner Self with guided meditations, scrapbooking, journaling, abstract painting and modelling clay. Vivienne loves to make baskets out of native Lomandra grass wrapped in colourful wool and usually has one or two craft projects on the go at any one time.

With an idea in mind, it is not uncommon for her to paint a canvas and then write the song and compose the music on her guitar to complete the artwork.

Vivienne is interested in people and their stories, and in particular the spawning point for all new ideas, and when she is not busy working at the Ultimate 48 Hour Author hub in Diamond Creek with Natasa and Stuart Denman, she can be found at the beach with her crafts.

Speaking about her menopausal journey, with the desire to inspire women around the world to embrace their bodies whilst making this significant change has now led Vivienne wanting to reach out to you all and ask the question, 'are you being kind to yourself?'

If the answer is 'Yes' – then more love and nurturing of yourself is food for the soul.

If the answer is No – then why not? It is time to peel your Onion.

Information on forthcoming workshops are available on her website.

Viviennemason.com

Onion Quotes

'Know your onions'.

'If you hear an onion ring, answer it.'
-**Anonymous**

'The onion and its satin wrappings are among the most beautiful of vegetables and is the only one that represents the essence of things. It can be said to have a soul.'
   ~ **My Summer in a Garden by Charles Dudley Warner**

'Onion skins very thin,
Mild winter coming in.
Onion skins very tough,
Coming winter very rough.'
~ **old English rhyme**

'It's probably illegal to make soups, stews and casseroles without plenty of onions.'
~ **Maggie Waldron, American author and editor**

'Life is like an onion.
You peel it off one layer at a time;
And sometimes you weep.'
~ **Carl Sandburg, American poet**

'Onions can make even heirs and widows weep.'
~ **Benjamin Franklin**

'Indeed, the tears live in an onion that should water this sorrow.'
~ **William Shakespeare quotes (English Dramatist, Playwright and Poet, 1564-1616)**

'It's toughest to forgive ourselves. So, it's probably best to start with other people. It's almost like peeling an onion. Layer by layer, forgiving others, you really do get to the point where you can forgive yourself.'
~ **Patty Duke**

Onion Tart

This recipe was cut out of a 'Marie Claire' magazine over 20 years ago and has been a top tart for many social gatherings as it is simple and delicious. The precious piece of paper is archived in one of many cookbooks in my sister's kitchen and I would like to dedicate this recipe to her.

As the pastry mixture is quite short, allow it to rest in the fridge for at least 15 minutes; it will be easier to roll and less likely to shrink during cooking. The pastry can be made up to three hours in advance and stored in the fridge, if wrapped in greaseproof paper.

Pastry:
- 350g plain flour
- 175g butter
- 2 egg yolks
- 2 tbsp cold water

Filling:
- 12 medium onions
  (use the red variety if you prefer)
- 125g butter
- 2 egg yolks
- Salt and freshly ground pepper

Cooking Method:

1. Sieve the flour into a large bowl, cut the butter into small chunks and rub into the flour with your fingertips until the mixture resembles coarse breadcrumbs. Beat the egg yolks with a fork, then stir them into the flour and butter. Sprinkle over 2 tablespoons cold water, or more as necessary, to bring the pastry together. Form the pastry into a ball, wrap in greaseproof paper and leave in the fridge for 15-20 minutes.

2. Peel the onions, and slice each from sprout to root into four segments. Melt the butter in a heavy-based pan on a low heat, add the onions and cook with a lid on, until golden and soft. This will take at least half an hour. Stir now and again to stop the onions sticking to the base of the pan. When they are cooked, season with a little salt and black pepper.

3. Preheat the oven to 200°C (gas mark 6). Remove the pastry from the fridge and roll out to fit a baking tray, 12 inches by 14 inches (30.4cm by 35.5 cm) or 13 inches by 13 inches (33cm square). Push the pastry into the corners with your fingertips; even if it doesn't reach up the sides of the tray, the filling should not spill out. Rest the pastry-filled tin in a cool place for 10 minutes.

4. When the onion mixture has cooled a little, stir in egg yolks, then spoon onto the pastry, spreading right up to the edges of the baking sheet. Bake for 35 minutes (40 minutes if necessary) until the onions are golden brown and the pastry edges crisp.

5. Cut the tart into squares and serve warm.

Enjoy!

www.ingramcontent.com/pod-product-compliance
Lightning Source LLC
Chambersburg PA
CBHW021108080526
44587CB00010B/438